WHERE THE FISH ARE

An Angler's Guide to Fish Behavior

DANIEL BAGUR

International Marine / McGraw-Hill

Camden, Maine New York Chicago San Francisco Lisbon London Madrid
Mexico City Milan New Delhi San Juan Seoul Singapore Sydney Toronto

The McGraw·Hill Companies

Library of Congress Cataloging-in-Publication Data

Bagur, Daniel.
    Where the fish are : an angler's guide to fish behavior / by Daniel Bagur.
      p.   cm.
    Includes bibliographical references and index.
    ISBN 978-0-07-159291-8 (alk. paper)
    1. Freshwater fishes—Behavior.   2. Freshwater fishes—Ecology.
  3. Freshwater fishes—Dispersal.   I. Title.

  QL624.B34   2009
  799.1′1—dc22   2008047896

1 2 3 4 5 6 7 8 9 10 11 12 13 14 15 16 17 18 19 20 21 22 23 24 25 26 27 28 29 FGR/FGR 0 9

ISBN 978-0-07-159291-8
MHID   0-07-159291-1

Interior photographs and artwork by Daniel Bagur

McGraw-Hill books are available at special quantity discounts to use as premiums and sales promotions or for use in corporate training programs. To contact a representative, please visit the Contact Us pages at www.mhprofessional.com.

This book is printed on acid-free paper.

I would like to dedicate this book to the town of Aberystwyth, Wales (where the bulk of it was written), and the fantastic group of friends I made there:

Cat Edwards, Dani Miller, Dave Adams, Dave Campbell, Gwilym Owen, Isabel Jones, Jon Fortnum, Joolz Fenton, Martin Holland, Nathan Robson, Paul Nuttall, Pete Evans, Pudre, Steve Watson, Susie Cox, Trudi Higginbotham, Vicky Stares, Willam Cullen

Ol' beauty

And, last but not least, to Bob Holtzman, my editor, without whom this book would still be just another file saved on my laptop

CONTENTS

Fishing in the Fish's World

The idea of this book came to me during a fishing trip. I was fly-fishing on a large freshwater lake when the weather turned. A heavy rainstorm moved toward me, casting a shadow over my boat. As the rain hammered down, the four flies I had laid just beneath the surface were taken within seconds by four fish. Was this a coincidence?

Every fisherman will remember a time when a change in the weather coincided with a surge or lull in fish feeding behavior. Whatever the species and whatever the weather event, there is no doubt about the dramatic and immediate influence weather can have on fishing action.

Weather forecasts are broadcast many times each day because of weather's influence on our own lives and behavior. The first thing we do in the morning is open the curtains and look at the weather. If this changeable factor is so important to us, with all our technological buffers, clothing, and shelter, it is easy to appreciate how significant it must be in the lives of wild animals, including fish. With climate change bringing even more dramatic weather extremes, the ability to read the impact of weather on fish is becoming an even more valuable tool to the angler.

Almost all animals have a much more refined ability to sense changing weather than we meteorologically blind humans. Relatively harsh extremes of weather may seem little more than beautiful displays when viewed from heated homes or cars. We react only when caught in the teeth of the most severe conditions, whereas fish are able to detect and adapt to the subtlest changes.

Even minor changes in a fish's immediate surroundings disrupt the fine equilibrium the fish maintains with its environment. These constant changes mean that the hot fishing spot of a few hours ago may now be empty water because the fish have moved elsewhere.

There is much debate in fishing magazines and along the riverbank about the exact influence of weather and other environmental variables on fish. While studying for my degree in marine and freshwater biology, I noticed that there was a great deal of information of use to anglers between the equations in the research papers I was reading. It is the aim of this book to replace rumors and opinion with facts revealed by scientific research. This understanding will give the reader a better knowledge of where fish are, and thus an enhanced ability to catch them. Scientific jargon has been kept to a minimum, and source references have been kept out of the text to make the content more accessible. A full list of sources can be found at the back of the book both to credit those who carried out the initial research and for those wishing to learn more about any given subject. Where an experiment is

What does it feel like to live in the fish's world?

mentioned in the text, full details can be found in the Notes section at the back of the book.

Meteorologists often get their weather predictions wrong, not because of faulty equipment or lack of expertise, but because the weather is influenced by so many variables that it is difficult with today's technology to measure and account for them all in a workable model. Similarly, any attempt to be dogmatic about fish behavior would be wrong given the dynamic nature of the subject. There are variations of behavior between one species and another and even between fish of the same species in different locations. There are few certainties, but, as we shall see, certain weather combinations encourage certain behaviors in certain species of fish. While knowledge of the factors influencing the location and feeding habits of fish will improve your fieldcraft and success, a large part of the pleasure of fishing is that there are rarely any guarantees. There are almost always exceptions to the rules.

In this book, we will examine how fish behave and think. We will look at the fishes' anatomy and sensory systems. The book covers fish welfare and the influence of light, oxygen, and temperature. We will discuss how weather changes such as wind, ice, rain, and snow can influence the behavior of fish. We will examine the impact of competition, predation, flooding, and seasonality on fish feeding.

As we will see, fish are significantly more intelligent than many people think. If the reader leaves this book with a greater respect for fish then my job will be done. Before we get into how fish react to changes within their environment, it is important to understand the animal we are dealing with. What would it be like to be a fish?

Understanding how fish think, and how they perceive and react to their environment, will make your angling more interesting and more successful.

CHAPTER *1*

How Fish Work, Behave, and Think

Fish are highly evolved creatures that have adapted to the aquatic environment physiologically and behaviorally over millions of years. The significant differences between their aquatic and our terrestrial worlds mean that fish are influenced by factors we may not even consider.

Knowledge of fish behavior and physiology is a vital part of an angler's skill set. Understanding how a fish works and what environmental cues fish are likely to be attracted to or repelled by enables an angler to put him- or herself into the fish's world, making every angling decision a little easier and improving the chances of a catch.

Of course, a reasonably complete overview of either fish behavior or anatomy alone would require a textbook in itself. What follows, therefore, is limited to those factors that have the greatest influence on angling.

Breathing and Metabolism

People use lungs to breathe air that, at ground level, has a more or less fixed and steady oxygen content. Fish, on the other hand, experience huge fluctuations in the levels of available oxygen. To make matters more complicated these fluctuations occur over relatively short time periods. These changes are due in part to the relationship between the temperature of water and its ability to hold oxygen. The warmer the water, the less oxygen it can hold.

Freshwater fish experience much higher oxygen fluctuations than their salt-water counterparts because it takes longer to heat or cool a larger volume of water. Smaller bodies of water, such as streams and small lakes, warm up and cool down more rapidly in response to the warming and cooling of the air and land around them.

Fish are well adapted to cope with these natural changes as they occur. Such changes do, however, influence where fish choose to spend their time and when they feed.

Gills

There are two main problems associated with obtaining oxygen from water. First, water contains less oxygen than air, around one-thirtieth as much per unit of volume. Second, water is denser than air. This makes it more difficult for fish to extract oxygen from water than it is for air breathers to extract oxygen from air. Through evolution, fish have gotten around these challenges by increasing the surface area of their respiratory organs and by pumping larger volumes of water over their respiratory surfaces.

A fish's gills are designed to expose as much surface area as possible to passing water, thereby maximizing the exchange of gasses between the fish's blood and the water. Each gill arch is covered by a strip of gill filaments, each filament is folded into a V shape to increase its surface area, and the filaments are covered in folds to further maximize their surface area. The membranes of the gill filaments are very thin, which further aids gas exchange. Species that lead more active lives, such as trout and bass, tend to have a greater number of gill filaments than less active species, providing them with the greater volume of oxygen needed to generate more energy.

As in humans, the red blood cells of fish contain a respiratory pigment called *hemoglobin*, which enables the blood to transport oxygen. Once the blood has passed through the gills, it is transported through the fish's body, where it provides the organs with their required oxygen.

The surface area of the gills is also used by fish to purge unwanted by-products of respiration from their blood. Carbon dioxide in the blood passes through the gill membranes and is absorbed by the surrounding water, while oxygen from the surrounding water passes through the membranes and is absorbed by the blood.

Water is pumped over the gills in two ways. Fish gulp a mouthful of water and then pump it into their gill chambers, where it passes over the gill filaments and back out into the environment. Some of the more active fish species, like bass and salmonids (including salmon, trout, char, and grayling), supplement this mechanism with another called *ram ventilation*. While swimming slowly or hovering at rest, fish pump water over their gills as described, but when swimming at speed, they open their mouths and allow water to "ram" through their gills, increasing the volume of oxygen available to the blood.

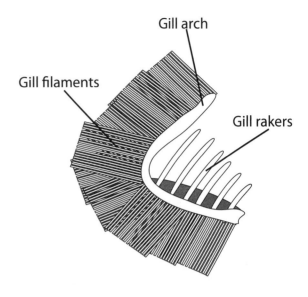

The gill structure of fish. The rakers filter out debris and keep it from damaging the filaments, where gas exchange between the fish's blood and the water occurs.

Metabolism

Wind strips heat from terrestrial animals in cold conditions much faster than cold air alone. In the same way, mammals swimming in fast-flowing water will lose heat faster than those in still water. For fish, this is not a problem, because fish are cold-blooded—that is, their body temperature rises and falls to remain in equilibrium with the surrounding water. This means that, unlike birds and mammals, fish do not need to expend energy maintaining their body temperature in a cold environment. This energy saving is highly advantageous, particularly in waters where temperatures fluctuate regularly.

During cold weather, fish simply reduce their activity levels. Since they do not need to waste energy maintaining their body temperature, they are able to feed less and keep still until temperatures return to more favorable levels. Because of this, fish seek out places that don't force them to waste energy during the winter. This often means moving into deeper water, where they can hide from predators and avoid currents that exist higher in the water column.

This behavioral pattern is mirrored somewhat by other species. Some aquatic insects, for example, burrow in pond mud when temperatures drop, enabling them to overwinter and survive for a number of years. Similarly, soil insects dig deeper, and tree beetles burrow beneath bark. The basic strategy used by these animals is to put as much distance and matter (be it mud, bark, or overlying water column) between themselves and the greatest extremes of cold. These creatures also move very little during the cold weather in order to conserve energy.

The range of temperatures fish can withstand is generally much smaller than that of terrestrial animals. This is because of the high rate of heat exchange between an aquatic animal and surrounding water. Terrestrial animals are surrounded by air, which has a lower rate of heat exchange, and can therefore survive low temperatures for longer.

Temperature further influences the feeding regimens of fish by determining the behavior of many of their prey species. This point can be illustrated in broad but graphic terms by considering the role of temperature in shark attacks on people. When the water is warm, people spend more time swimming and venture farther from shore. This behavior raises the encounter rate between human swimmers and sharks, and as a result, the number of mistaken attacks increases.

The situation is similar for freshwater fish. Temperatures affect the behavior of the invertebrates upon which these fish feed in a way that influences encounter rates between them and their food. As a general rule, the warmer the water, the greater the activity levels of invertebrates and the higher the level of feeding activity by fish, which in turn increases encounter rates between foraging fish and predatory ones.

Tight Lines
The level of a fish's hunger can influence its position within the water column.

The level of a fish's hunger can influence its position within the water column (the position of the fish vertically in the water). Hungry fish seek out water that is a few degrees cooler than that preferred by fish that have finished feeding, and of course, deeper waters tend to be cooler. Hungry fish also move around more looking for food and therefore take more risks than fish that are full.

Along the coast, mackerel tend to be more abundant when colder bottom layers are covered by warmer surface waters. This is because mackerel prefer feeding in colder, deeper layers during the day and rising into warmer layers at night, when they are not feeding. The warmer water aids their digestion.

In the middle and high latitudes of the Northern Hemisphere, the highest water temperatures occur in July, August, and September, and the lowest in February and March. Seasonal temperature changes tend to occur slowly, while daily changes in the weather can be much faster, reducing the time available for fish to adapt. Changes in water temperature follow several hours behind changes in the air. During rapid temperature changes in fresh water, fish often go deep, where temperatures are more constant.

Because of their reduced activity levels in cold temperatures, fish eat less, and in fact, trout stop growing below 6°C (43°F). Given the prevailing water temperatures in their normal habitats, this means that most wild brown trout spend about half their lives not growing. There is a chicken-and-egg aspect to this, for when fish eat less, they become less active in order to conserve energy and therefore need less to eat, so they forage less, which conserves energy, and so on.

Like humans, fish do "snack" between meals, but with less intensity than they show at mealtime. If the opportunity for an easy meal occurs, a fish will break its fast and take the morsel. When temperatures are low and fish are trying to conserve energy, they require a greater temptation to stir them from their torpor. Cold weather therefore calls for the use of larger baits, both to provide that additional temptation and to be visible from a longer distance to fish that are not moving much. When temperatures are higher, small baits should be used, as they are less likely to be inspected carefully and rejected during periods of high feeding activity.

Along ocean coasts during the summer, when the weather is good, shallow waters are warmed by the air then cooled by incoming tides. As the tide falls again, the waters are once again heated by the sun. In winter the reverse occurs. Freezing temperatures cool shallow waters, then the incoming tide raises them. As the tide ebbs once more, the shallow water begins to cool again. Coastal fish will almost always feed during a rising tide. This is because it quickly exposes new and plentiful feeding grounds. The advantages to be gained from feeding during the incoming tide generally outweigh the problems of fluctuating temperature and exposure to predators. Fish feeding on the incoming tide can be found just behind the tide line in very shallow water. In extreme cases, their backs will appear above the water.

Energy Budget

Each species of fish behaves in accordance with its characteristic energy budget, which is a calculation of the amount

> **Tight Lines**
> Fish feeding on the incoming tide can be found just behind the tide line in very shallow water.

of energy a fish has available for growth and reproduction. It takes into account the quantity and quality of food consumed and the energy lost as heat through metabolic processes and in fecal pellets and other excretory products.

Although these calculations are of little direct use to anglers, they illustrate a highly useful concept: wild fish often behave in ways that conserve energy. They have evolved to instinctively balance the energy gain of a meal against the energy loss in terms of pursuing, catching, and consuming the meal (as well as the risk of predation while seeking the meal). Trout, for example, often hide behind rocks to shield themselves from stream flow, darting out into the full force of the current only when a large enough morsel of food passes by. As we shall see, this does not mean that larger flies, lures, and baits are always better. When food is abundant and fish have ample energy reserves, they can become fussy about what and when they eat, and a smaller, better-presented bait, lure, or fly may be a more favorable option. It is, however, important for anglers to consider how much energy fish are likely to have at any given time, and to fish accordingly. For example, in the cold of winter, fish try to conserve their energy and are less likely to travel for a meal. At these times, an angler must do the traveling and cover plenty of water to find fish.

The energy budget also highlights other important aspects of angling, such as speed of retrieval. When fish are conserving energy because of low temperatures, slower retrieves are more likely to get a bite because the lethargic fish will have more time to spot and intercept a passing hook.

Tight Lines
Wild fish often behave in ways that conserve energy, making slow retrieves more effective in low temperatures.

One experiment done in 1984 clearly highlights the importance of the principle of energy conservation to anglers. Through an aquarium with curved sides to imitate a stream channel, water was recirculated to create an artificial current. The researcher placed stones in strategic positions and manipulated the sediment to create microhabitats, then he "stocked" the aquarium—first with coho salmon, then brown trout, and finally brook trout, clipping the fins of the fish to identify individuals.

In each case he left the fish in place long enough for growth to occur. One difference among the three species was that while the brown and brook trout used their pectoral fins to grip the bottom of the tank during periods of high water velocity, the coho salmon never rested on the bottom at any point. The subordinate (weaker) trout would hide, lodging themselves between the Plexiglas wall of the "stream" and the gravel. The dominant fish in all species would consistently retain the most profitable positions within the stream—that is, the positions requiring the least expenditure of energy (behind stones, for example) and with the best food supply (close to a fast current). Growth rates for fish corresponded to their positions. Those in the best positions grew fastest, those in less profitable positions grew more slowly, and some were forced to settle for positions in which they actually lost weight. Understanding where fish prefer to live will lead you to the biggest individuals.

Scales and Skin

A fish's skin, like human skin, is designed to protect the organism from the environment. Fish skin contains glands that cover the fish with a film of mucus, which helps protect the skin from disease and parasites. In any catch-and-release fishery, care must be taken to avoid removing this mucus and thus exposing the fish to potential illnesses.

> **Tight Lines**
> Trout can camouflage themselves, getting darker or lighter according to their background. Knowing what shade or color you're looking for can be helpful.

A little-known fact about many fish is that they can change the color of their skin, camouflaging themselves against their background. Trout, for example, gradually release melanin into skin cells when swimming over a dark riverbed or in peaty water, making themselves darker. Over a light background, they reduce their melanin levels, and their skin becomes lighter. Paling of the skin is controlled by nervous impulses and occurs rapidly, while the darkening process is controlled hormonally and is therefore slower. The trout's sense of sight is vital to these short-term color changes; blind trout are unable to make such alterations. It is useful for anglers to be aware of these adaptations when trying to spot trout in shallow water. It can help if you know what shade or color you are looking for.

Take care not to damage the fish's skin or the mucous film that it secretes.

Embedded within the skin are the scales, which provide physical protection. Fish scales grow slowly during the winter and more rapidly in summer. This leads to an increase or decrease in the calcium deposits laid down in ridges known as *circuli* on the scales. The comparatively thinly spaced circuli of winter can be used to count the number of years a fish has been alive, much like the annual rings of a tree. The thickness of these rings can also be used to assess growth rates at particular stages within a fish's life cycle.

Other calcified structures within the body of a fish can be used in much the same way. *Otoliths* are found in the inner ears of fish, each ear containing three. These structures show a daily cycle of periods when calcium is more rapidly deposited, as opposed to the seasonal one shown by scales. This daily cycle is of particular use in determining the age of very young fish. For catfish, the pectoral spines can also be used. The obvious disadvantage of utilizing otoliths and pectoral spines is that the fish must be killed in order for its age and growth rates to be determined. In contrast, a few scales can be removed from a live fish without causing too much damage. It is important to determine the age of a fish at a given size to discover the growth rate. In some fisheries fish grow slowly and in others they grow quickly. This can be due to many factors such as the availability of food, competition, temperature, and so on. This information is of use to anglers because fish grow much bigger in some waters than in others.

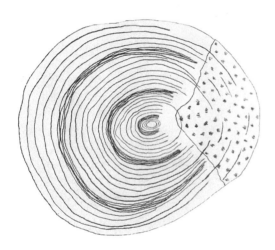

A fish scale. The mottled, pie-slice-shaped section is the visible part of the scale on the fish. The roughly concentric curves are *circuli*, indicating growth of the scale. Slow growth during winter results in tight spacing of the circuli, called an *annulus*, each annulus indicating one winter of the fish's life.

Moving in Three Dimensions

Fish live in a three-dimensional world, moving and holding position both horizontally and vertically. They use different mechanisms for these two axes of motion: their muscles for the horizontal and their swim bladders for the vertical.

Muscles and Skeleton

The swimming and fighting power of fish comes from their lateral muscle structures (called *myotomes*), which are situated along a fish's sides. As the muscles on one side contract, they shorten that side of the fish. The fish's skeletal system provides support so that the muscle contraction pulls the fish's tail toward the contracting side. By alternating contractions on one side with contractions on the other, the fish swishes its tail from side to side, and the fish swims. Depending on the species, these muscles can contribute the bulk of the fish's overall weight—as much as 70 percent in salmonids. It is these muscles that we eat when we catch fish for the table.

A fossil from millions of years ago shows the skeleton of a fish.

Broadly, these muscles are of two types. *White muscle* is fueled anaerobically (without oxygen) by chemical energy stores within the muscle tissue. These muscles are used for bursts of speed but tire quickly and require rest. *Red muscles*, which are fueled by oxygen (aerobic power), are used for swimming at cruising speeds and are found in greater amounts nearer the tail of the fish. Using these muscles, fish can swim quite happily at two body lengths per second for extended periods of time. In most fish, these muscles make up around 10 percent of the muscle mass.

It is the white muscles that are likely to cause an angler problems. When an angler hooks a fish, the quarry bursts into a run, then slows again as the high-speed (white) muscles tire. The fish then reduces activity before building up the energy to make another full-speed dash. There are two times when you're playing a fish that this dash is particularly likely. One is when the fish first feels the resistance of the line after being hooked. It will respond by trying to escape from the pull of the line and swim at high speed in the opposite direction. The second time is when the fish first sees you as it approaches the surface.

It is important to be ready for a white-muscle burst at all times, particularly when catching more active species such as salmon, trout, and bass. Always ensure that the reel is set to pay off fishing line if the fish makes a dash.

Rheotaxis

Fish prefer to point their heads into the flow of the water. This behavior is referred to as *rheotaxis*, and it's as logical as a powerboater's preference to approach a dock against rather than with the current. Fish, like boats, don't move effectively in reverse, so if a fish wishes simply to hold position in flowing water, its only option is to swim forward at the speed of the current that is moving against it.

When fishing in flowing water, always cast upstream of the fish and allow the bait to travel downstream toward it. This will present the bait in front of the fish and allow it plenty of time to spot and move to intercept the meal. In faster water, use larger flies and baits; at lower speeds, use a smaller fly or bait. A fish has less time to inspect an offering that is moving fast, and for this reason, the take will often be hard-hitting in faster water. Use strong line to avoid breakage. In slower or still water, a fish may inspect a bait or fly closely before deciding whether or not to eat, so a good presentation is important.

> **Tight Lines**
> When fishing in flowing water, always cast upstream of the fish and allow the bait to travel downstream toward it.

Swim Bladder

In the aquatic environment, depth provides a third dimension not readily accessible to humans, and fish have adapted to particular depths within the water col-

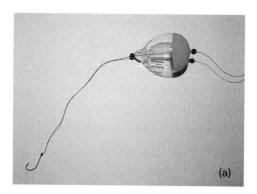 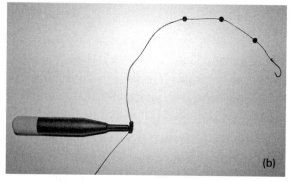

(a) In slow-flowing water, bait has time to sink and therefore does not require any additional weight. (b) In a faster current, add some shot to the hook length to ensure that it sinks to where the fish are feeding.

umn. To put it simply, a given species of fish will concentrate itself at certain depths at certain times. Fish choose depths that put them in their preferred temperatures and their preferred levels of oxygen and light, and they move up and down with the weather, time of day, and season.

Fish hold their vertical position in the water column using a swim bladder. *Physostomous* fish, those in which a duct connects the swim bladder with the alimentary canal, can swallow air at the water's surface and pass it into the bladder in order to float, and they can sink by "burping" out unwanted gas. *Physoclistous* fish, in contrast, swallow air to fill their bladder for the first time as larvae, and by adulthood, the swim bladder is sealed, and its volume of gas is controlled by gas resorption and excretion mechanisms. These mechanisms can work quickly to compensate for pressure changes, but physoclistous fish still cannot change the volume of gas in their swim bladder as quickly as physostomous fish can and are therefore less likely to make significant depth changes to intercept an angler's hook. Gauging the correct depth for such a species is therefore more important. Bass, walleye, and perch are physoclistous; carp, salmon, and trout are physostomous.

Pressure changes rapidly with even slight changes in depth. A pressure decrease of 60 percent is experienced by a fish moving from a depth of 7 meters (23 feet) to the water's surface, and that's enough to rupture the swim bladder and kill a significant number of physoclistous (unable to "burp") fish. It would take physoclistous fish several minutes to acclimate to such a change, so it's essential to be careful when catching fish in deeper water. Allow the fish time to acclimate and do not just pump it to the surface, since you won't know for certain whether you've hooked a physostomous or a physoclistous fish until it's in sight.

Bigger fish will ordinarily fight hard and take longer to land, and therefore have longer to acclimate while they're fighting. Even large fish, however, may lack energy in certain conditions, as in cold weather. Below 8°C (46°F), fish tend to tire more quickly.

A common misconception among anglers is that if a fish looks OK when it is returned to the water, it will survive. This is not always the case. Fish that have been overstressed or badly damaged—and a ruptured swim bladder certainly qualifies as severe damage—can sink to the bottom and die.

> *Tight Lines*
> For catch and release, know that quickly pulling certain fish to the surface from deep water might rupture their swim bladders and eventually kill them, even if they look OK when set free.

Spawning Behavior

The spawning times of fish are important for anglers. Fish are larger and in better condition prior to spawning. They often lose considerable weight during spawning, and many species migrate to new habitats and are therefore not to be found in their usual locations. It is also important that anglers respect the closed season for their chosen species, allowing the fish to spawn in peace.

Spawning Seasons for Common Game Fish

Time of Year	Species
Early spring	Northern pike
Spring	Chain pickerel, rainbow trout, redfin pickerel, yellow perch, sauger, walleye, cutthroat trout, largemouth bass, smallmouth bass, spotted bass, redeye bass, black crappie, white crappie, bluegill, white perch, yellow bass, white bass, striped bass, paddlefish
Middle to late spring	Muskellunge
Late spring	White sturgeon
Late spring to early summer	Warmouth, rock bass, Sacramento perch, pumpkinseed, redear sunfish, green sunfish, white catfish, flathead catfish, yellow bullhead, brown bullhead, shovelnose sturgeon, lake sturgeon, blue catfish, channel catfish, black bullhead, redbreast sunfish
Summer	Mountain trout, arctic char, longear sunfish
Late summer to early fall	Sockeye salmon, brook trout, bull trout
Fall	Chinook salmon, cisco (i.e., lake herring), inconnu, chum salmon, brown trout, Atlantic salmon, lake trout, bull char, coho salmon, pink salmon
Late fall to early winter	Lake whitefish

Prior to their spawning times, game fish will move from their preferred year-round habitats into their spawning grounds. Various species have particular requirements for their feeding and spawning grounds, as shown in the following table.

Feeding and Spawning Habitats, by Species

Species	Feeding Ground	Spawning Ground
Arctic grayling, ciscoes, and inconnu	Clear, oligotrophic (with a poor nutrient supply) lakes or rivers	Well-oxygenated, gravel-bottomed streams or tributaries
Mountain and lake whitefish	Deeper areas of slow-flowing waters	Highly oxygenated gravel riffles in nearby streams
Pink, chinook, Atlantic, chum, sockeye, and coho salmon and golden, rainbow, lake, and brown trout	Deeper stretches of rivers or lakes	Upstream to more highly oxygenated gravel riffles of streams or inlets
Arctic char	Deep water of cold lakes	Rocky margins of the lake
Largemouth, smallmouth, and rock bass	Eutrophic (with a plentiful nutrient supply), vegetated lakes	Shallow margins of these lakes
Northern pike, muskellunge, chain pickerel, and yellow perch	Deeper regions in weedy natural lakes and rivers	Margins of these water bodies
Blue and channel catfish	Large rivers	Holes or beneath tree roots on the river's bank

Some species of fish cease feeding during the spawning period and can be more difficult to catch. Atlantic cod, for example, stop feeding on average thirty-six days before spawning and begin feeding rapidly again after the release of the last batch of eggs. Atlantic salmon notoriously refuse to feed just before entering their home river. They will not feed at all during their freshwater migration. Anglers know that the salmon will, however, snap at attractor flies on their way up the spawning beds.

Ecomorphology

You can learn a great deal just by looking at the fish you are trying to catch. What an animal looks like is closely correlated with the environment in which it has evolved. Scientists call this relationship the *ecomorphological hypothesis*.

Evolution is driven by natural selection. Mutations and the mixing of genes during sexual reproduction cause genetic variations. Most of these changes are useless, and some are even harmful. (For example, genetic mutations and gene mixing can make individuals more prone to disease or can result in physical deformities.) Occasionally, however, a random change gives an animal an advantage over its rivals, perhaps making it better at catching prey or escaping predators. The higher survival rate that such a mutation confers might enable this individual to have more offspring than others, thus passing on its advantageous genetic trait to its young. This process ensures that those organisms that are best adapted to their environments are more common in future generations. It is important to note that such changes typically take place over millions of years.

What constitutes an advantageous trait, however, is defined by the environment in which the organism lives. A fish living in a pitch-dark cave, for example, would not benefit from having slightly larger eyes, but one living in the middle of the water column might well benefit from enhanced eyesight at low levels of illumination. This adaptation might enable the fish to hunt more effectively or detect threats sooner. In this environment, the inherited trait of the larger eye might help that individual survive longer and thereby improve its chances of reproducing.

Because water is much denser than air, fish have to overcome more drag (friction with the surrounding water) than animals that walk on land or fly. It is clear when you look at the shape of a fish that its body has been constructed to allow it to move easily within the aquatic environment. A torpedo-shaped body slides with relative ease through the viscous medium in which fish live. In fact, all fast-moving aquatic life is greatly streamlined to reduce drag through this thick medium. The faster the water velocity in which a fish lives, the more streamlined the fish needs to be. Not surprisingly, aquatic mammals, such as whales and dolphins, that live in a similar environment and with similar requirements for survival have bodies similar to fish.

Structures of rock and vegetation in the fish's habitat are also important. Where there are more nooks, crannies, and obstacles to maneuver among, fish have evolved deeper (comparatively taller in height) bodies because this shape is ideal for turning quickly and sharply (the extra height acts as a rudder). This is a common characteristic of prey fish that live in weed beds, where agility is more important than straight-ahead speed when dodging and hiding from predators. Prey fish that live in open water, on the other hand, need to be faster to avoid predation (as do their predators in order to catch them). Their bodies are somewhat rounder in cross section, making them more torpedo-shaped overall and increasing their speed potential at the expense of maneuverability.

Tight Lines
The mouths, teeth, and jaws of fish tell us a great deal about their lives.

A fish's surroundings have other influences. If the background consists of brown rocks, for example, the fish, be it predator or prey, might benefit from being brown as well, making it less likely to be seen. Fish living amid rocks often remain motionless to avoid detection by predators, while those living in weed beds are less conspicuous among the swaying stems and can therefore move more freely without being seen. Again, this information is useful when you decide how to fish your chosen bait in a chosen location.

The mouths, teeth, and jaws of fish also tell us a great deal about their world and provide useful hints about how and where to catch them. The position and shape of a fish's mouth, for instance, is an indicator of where it feeds. Fish that feed primarily on the surface often have a short upper lip and a long lower lip, thus angling the mouth upward. This facilitates feeding on the surface film of the water and reduces the chances that the potential meal will evade capture. Bottom-feeders show the reverse, with a protruding upper lip angling the mouthparts downward. Those with sensory barbells hanging from their mouthparts often feed in the sediment on the bottom. Generalist feeders like trout have a fairly even mouth that enables them to feed at the surface or on the bottom.

Many predators such as northern pike, pickerel, and muskellunge have long, pincerlike jaws, which enable them to lunge at their prey and trap it in their mouths, and inwardly inclined teeth to prevent live prey from escaping. Fish such as warmouth that eat hard-shelled creatures, such as snails, have flattened teeth adapted for crushing. Insectivorous fish, including trout, have small, needlelike teeth to help trap their insect prey.

This young brown trout's small, sharp teeth reflect its preference for invertebrate prey. Note also its prominent lateral line, discussed later in this chapter.

Even the length of a fish's gut can provide insight into the food it eats. Plant matter

Tight Lines
Be sure to take into account what and how a fish eats to determine what methods you use. Fish that hunt other fish are best lured by the imitation of prey, insect-eaters by flies, and bottom-feeding scavengers by dead bait.

is harder to digest than animal protein, and as a result, carnivores have much shorter digestive tracts than herbivores. Omnivorous animals have medium-length digestive tracts.

If we know what and how a fish eats, that can tell us a great deal about what fishing method to use. If the species actively hunts other fish as prey, for example, use a lure that visually imitates prey fish. Insect-eaters are likely to go after flies, and bottom-feeding scavengers often strike at dead baits.

We can take this idea further and use it to discover if there are any predators about. Certain aquatic animals, like stickleback, are covered with heavy, armored plates or spearlike projections along their sides or back. Such adaptations represent a major investment from the fish's energy budget and are often detrimental in such day-to-day activities as foraging or swimming. Interestingly, the amount of armor evolved has been shown to correlate closely with the level of predator threat within the ecosystem. Since preventing themselves from being eaten by scavengers after they die is useless to fish, such defenses would only evolve where predators hunting live prey are present. The presence of such defensive structures is thus a sure sign that efficient predators shared the waters that the animal in question evolved in. Predators, of course, are often favored game fish, so use these signs accordingly. But note that predatory fish often avoid heavily defended species in preference of others. The defensive spines of a stickleback, for example, might give clues about the presence of desirable predatory fish, but stickleback might not make good bait because the local predators are likely to know from experience that those spines don't go down well. The angler should therefore choose a less well-defended species as bait.

We can also get clues about where fish prefer to spend their time by looking at their sensory systems. Fish with large eyes are likely to hunt by sight and live in well-lit habitats. Fish with small eyes and large barbells—like catfish—are more likely to spend their time in darker habitats, using their senses of taste and touch to detect prey.

Ecomorphology is not an exact science, and there are frequent exceptions to the "rules." It can, however, provide you with an excellent head start. You can tell what a fish is likely to feed on and what kind of habitat it may live in simply by looking at it. You can also find clues about the presence of predatory fish, what bait to select, and even how to fish that bait. This information is particularly useful to novice anglers or when you're fishing far from home with little knowledge of the habits of local species. A fish must be seen before this information can be used, but a photograph can be as useful as the real thing.

Fish Senses

Of all a fish's adaptations to its environment, none is more relevant to fishing tactics than its senses. It is by sight, sound, smell, taste, and touch that fish seek food and avoid predators. The essence of fishing is little more than attempting to replicate stimuli the target species relies upon to identify food while avoiding the appearance of stimuli the fish will interpret as signs of predators.

Sight

The perceptual world of animals is often strikingly different from our own, and few animals live in a world more different from ours than fish. Their eyes show a greater variety of adaptations than those of terrestrial animals because of the constantly varying light conditions in the aquatic environment. Fish are primarily visual predators, and a large part of their brain is devoted to sight. As a result, many species are often relatively inactive during darkness.

The optic lobes comprise the greatest part of a fish's brain because most fish are primarily visual predators.

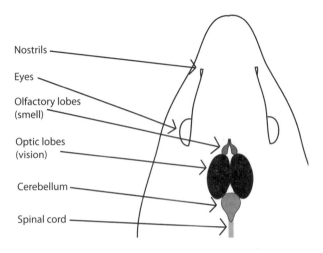

Nostrils

Eyes

Olfactory lobes (smell)

Optic lobes (vision)

Cerebellum

Spinal cord

Most fish hunt by sight and use their sense of vision to avoid predators.

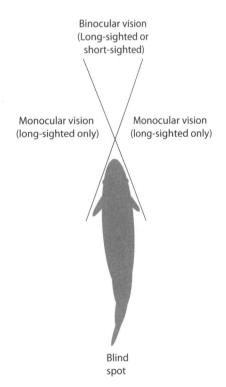

Binocular vision (Long-sighted or short-sighted)

Monocular vision (long-sighted only)

Monocular vision (long-sighted only)

Blind spot

With their eyes mounted on the sides of the head, fish can see almost all the way around themselves.

The human eye is able to view only a small area of focus at a time, but if we need to change our field of view moderately, we rotate our eyes in their sockets, and if we need to change the field of view significantly, we turn our heads. Fish have a comparatively limited ability to move their eyeballs, and their "necks" are also comparatively immobile, so their eyes have evolved to compensate by vastly increasing the angle of their visual field. Fish can view almost the whole of the underwater horizon, with the exception of a blind spot directly behind and below them. In front, the visual fields of both eyes overlap, providing an area of binocular vision. This allows a feeding fish to accurately judge the distances of prey items. Simultaneously, fish are able to use monocular vision to monitor the horizon on each flank and many degrees to the rear for the presence of food or predators.

When fish peer through the water's surface, they see our world through "Snell's window," which describes the fish's field of view above the water's surface. On a calm day with flat water, the radius of this window is approximately the same as the fish's depth. Under these conditions, an angler's lure, fly, or bait cast onto the surface will be seen by a fish swimming five feet below the surface only if it is within five feet of the fish's horizontal position. Around this window, the fish sees a silvery reflection of the river or lake bed, along with whatever else is swimming in the water nearby.

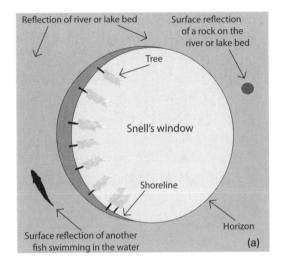

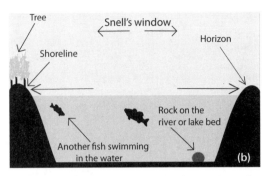

"Snell's window" describes the fish's view of the world above the surface of the water. At left (a) is the fish's view through the window; above (b) is a conventional side view of the same scene showing the fish in relation to its surroundings.

Fish at greater depths have a larger window, but the objects seen through it are darker and more blurred. It is, therefore, always a good idea to cast a bait directly above the fish. Objects appear larger in the center of the window and are less likely to be confused with the land, anglers, and trees bunched up along the window's edges. It is important to note here that fish can also see other underwater objects around them as they observe the view above with the sky as a background.

When fish leave the water, as happens when they leap or are caught, the different light properties of air render the fish momentarily nearsighted. Normal vision is restored immediately when a fish returns to the water.

In general, the bigger the eye, the more light it can collect and the more sensitive it will be. (Giant squid have eyes the size of your head, and it is theorized that this enables them to detect very low levels of bioluminescence made by other species, especially their prey, in the great depths at which they live.) Light sensitivity also depends on the density of visual pigments in the eye, with greater pigment density permitting detection of lower levels of light. Both characteristics are evolutionary adaptations to a fish's environmental niche and its behavioral needs.

As in humans, the layer of light-sensitive cells lining the eyeball or retina of a fish contains both rod and cone cells. Rod cells cannot perceive color but are more sensitive and work better under low-light conditions. Cone cells are able to

> **Tight Lines**
> When fish leave the water, the different light properties of air make them nearsighted.

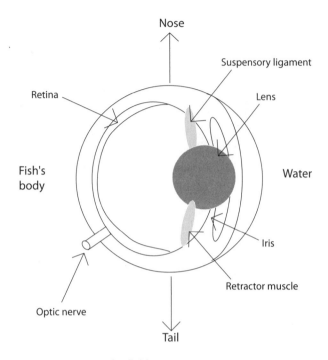

Basic structure of a fish's eye.

differentiate colors but require the brightness of sunlight to function properly. As a fish grows, the numbers of rods and cones within its eyes increase, resulting in an increase in visual acuity and sensitivity with age. The greater the visual acuity, the greater the range at which a fish can see a given object. This improvement occurs most rapidly during the early stages of the fish's growth, then slows down toward adulthood. Bigger fish are therefore better able to detect badly presented bait.

At rest, a fish's eye is nearsighted toward the front and farsighted to the side. (This is because fluid pressure within the eye pushes the fish's spherical lens forward.) This enables fish to pick off small prey items swimming close in front of them while keeping an eye on the distant horizon for more food or approaching predators.

Although a fish's eyes cannot be focused as efficiently as our own, fish are able to pull the lens back toward their tail using a muscle within the eye. As the lens is moved, the side view remains the same while the front view also becomes farsighted. This enables the fish to focus on items at varying distances in front of it while checking the distant horizon on its flanks at all times.

Fish do not have eyelids and cannot dilate their pupils as fast or as much as humans. This means they are less able to control the amount of light entering the eye. They protect their eyes by moving deeper on brighter days.

In addition to their eyes, fish employ another "visual" organ, the *pineal body*. This light-sensitive organ is situated at the top of the brain and skull, beneath a thin layer of bone. It is used to detect dusk and dawn and is therefore of importance to the fish's circadian rhythm (i.e., its "body clock"). It is also used to detect shadows moving above, warning of potential danger. You should thus avoid casting shadows over the water while you fish. It is likely to spook the fish and put them off their feed.

Visual Acuity

Due to the light-absorbing and light-scattering properties of water, it is unlikely that fish are able to focus clearly on anything but the closest of objects. The farther an object is from a fish, the more severely the details of its image are degraded by scattering light. Generally speaking, the distance from which a fish reacts to objects of interest (such as your hook bait) increases with light level and is thus much greater during sunny days than cloudy days or at night.

> **Tight Lines**
> Generally, fish will react to hook bait from farther distances on sunny days.

Fresh water is often far from clear. Surrounded by land, it is filled with minute plant and animal life, reducing its visual clarity. The clearest water tends to be oceanic and located well away from land and the effects of river-mouth silting, organic runoff, and shallow, wave-driven turbidity.

Fish are unlikely to see objects beyond 40 meters even in the clearest of waters—including ocean waters far offshore and "gin-clear" chalk streams—and 6 to 9 meters is the common limit for visual clarity in some freshwater environments. It is important to note here that when fish look upward, their visual range increases. This is because downwelling light silhouettes objects above the fish, causing them to stand out more clearly against the sky.

Beyond their visual distance limits, other senses come into play, and fish often locate prey by other sensory means before locking in, using sight as they get nearer. Often an angler must get a fish's attention from a distance with bright colors, noise, and smell while also presenting a bait that is enticing and convincing under closer scrutiny. You must consider which sense to aim for when attracting fish. Weather conditions, as we shall see, play a vital role in this decision-making process.

At close range, fish see fine details and are likely to appreciate a well-tied fly or be spooked by highly visible line or bulky knots. When a fish makes a speedy attack, however, as during lure-fishing, such details are unlikely to be important. The distance between the fish and the lure at the moment the fish decides to strike

Tight Lines
Ensure that everything
looks natural when
using static baits that
can be scrutinized; for
fast retrieves, there
is less need to worry
about the presentation.

is likely to be too great for it to notice such details, and the speed, retrieve, and strike subsequently blur any fine details. In short, if you're using a fast retrieve, don't worry too much about the presentation. If you are using static baits that fish can approach and scrutinize, try to ensure that everything looks natural.

Color Vision

Given the vast variety of colors in which fish are clothed, it makes sense that fish have evolved color vision to use this additional sensory stimulus. Indeed, color is widely used by fish to recognize school mates, predators, and prey, as well as during courtship displays. Because fish are less able to perceive the detailed outline of an object from a distance, it is likely that color and contrast play an important role in object recognition.

The most famous example of this is Niko Tinbergen's description of the reaction of his stickleback to the postman's mail van. Male stickleback are highly territorial and develop deep red coloration during the spawning season. Tinbergen kept a male stickleback in a tank by the window. He noticed that when the red mail van passed along the road outside, his stickleback would become highly aggressive, attacking the side of the tank in an attempt to scare off the van! The fact that the stickleback did not react this way when the white milk van drove past is good evidence for color awareness in fish.

Male stickleback use color to communicate during the spawning season.

In behavioral experiments designed to test a fish's ability to distinguish among colors including ultraviolet light, fish are trained to respond to a light source and are rewarded with food for approaching it. When two light sources are presented, the fish is rewarded for approaching a light of a particular color. If fish are able to choose one color consistently over other colors, even when lights are shuffled in the aquarium, then the fish must be able to differentiate among the colors. By increasing the number and types of colors in the experiment, it is possible to discover which colors a particular species of fish is sensitive to.

In her excellent book *Through Our Eyes Only?*, Marian Stamp Dawkins describes how fish can be automatically rewarded for swimming through certain hoops placed in their tanks. A photobeam is used to pick up the fish as it passes, and food is automatically released. This kind of experiment can be taken to the next level by encouraging the fish to swim through an increasing number of colored hoops to get different types of food. In this way, it is possible to "ask" the fish which food it prefers by observing which food it will do the most work to obtain.

As well as having color vision, fish are able to detect light that we humans are unable to see. Ultraviolet light has a short wavelength (shorter than 400 nanometers), too short for the human eye to perceive. Several surface-dwelling fish species, including juvenile brown and rainbow trout, have cones sensitive to ultraviolet light. These ultraviolet-sensitive cones are thought to be lost as trout mature into adults.

Why do trout lose their ultraviolet sensitivity? The scattering of ultraviolet light means that it is only of use within the first few meters of the water column and that it can only be used to see in detail at close range. While young fry live in shallow, sunlit waters and hunt for food over small distances, adult trout migrate into deeper water and lose the need for ultraviolet vision. Also, since there is a cost to the use of ultraviolet light—in that it would damage the retina if allowed to pass through the lens—trout apparently block it out as they get older.

Which colors make the best flies and lures? In fresh water, red is the most easily visible color, since it has a long wavelength and is scattered the least. It would make sense, therefore, to include flecks of red on flies and lures. These flecks would attract the attention of a fish from the maximum possible distance (around 9 meters). You needn't worry much about the exact color of an imitative pattern, since individuals of the same prey species often differ slightly in color tone themselves.

Adding a red tag or mark to a spoon will increase the odds of its being spotted.

Many fish identify specific prey by their appearance, and lures are available that imitate a variety of prey species.

Size, Shape, and Movement

A fish's eye is highly sensitive to movement. Juvenile fish in particular respond to movement more than size or shape. Adult fish are more complicated. For example, salmonids feed on animals, such as freshwater snails, that remain motionless for long periods, and in such instances, fish seem to select prey on the basis of size, shape, and color. Sometimes fish will only feed when they see prey items conforming to a detailed and specific visual pattern, while at other times they will chase any object that is moving.

Movement has other advantages to anglers, of course; moving bait will cover more water and therefore come within sight of more feeding fish. Predators are more likely to attack fish that are unaware of their presence than those that have become wary upon spotting them. Prey fishes' heightened awareness makes them more difficult to catch. During the fry season, for example, when you are imitating a fry in order to catch large trout, try to make it look ill or weak with a jerky, seemingly uncontrolled retrieve. Floating fry either left static or twitched along the surface work well because they look like injured fish. Similarly, if you present a lure so as to resemble a fish that is unaware of its surroundings and therefore likely to make an easier meal than its school mates, you may encourage a predatory fish to make a lunge for it.

Experiments have shown that visual contrast is another vital factor both for predators and for prey. One of the reasons pike stalk prey successfully is their mottled, low-contrast colors. Prey fish simply don't notice the predators' presence until too late. On the other hand, predators often rely on visual contrast to identify their prey. For anglers, the lesson is simple: it can be a mistake to blend a fly with the background. Try to mimic natural odors, with a twist. Make your flies and baits stand out, and provide the target fish with an irresistibly easy meal.

> **Tight Lines**
> Make your flies and baits stand out to provide the target fish with an irresistibly easy meal.

Because underwater conditions vary so greatly, it is difficult to give specific advice about which color to use under which circumstances. There are general rules, however:

- ▸ In clear water, the most visible colors are fluorescent blue and white.
- ▸ In colored water, the most visible colors are fluorescent yellow and fluorescent green or blue.
- ▸ At dawn and dusk, in muddy water, or when light levels are low, it is better to use fluorescent colors rather than metallic lures, as metallics rely on the reflection of sunlight, whereas fluorescents provide their own brightness.

Plastics, woods, and metals hold paint well and thus make easily seen lure materials underwater. Other materials such as hairs, feathers, and softer synthetics used to tie flies and lures can often be more difficult for fish to see for two reasons. First, lures and flies are designed by tackle manufacturers to catch anglers first and fish second. A shiny new lure with bright tufts of vivid color is impossible to miss in the tackle shop, but once it has been cast a few times, the color of the soft materials may fade, and the accumulation of dirt from the water may further reduce its visibility. Also, when large, bushy tails get wet, they stick together and become thin streaks that are much less likely to be seen than the brand-new (and dry) fly or lure may suggest.

If in doubt, buy or tie flies with painted plastic or metallic beads. These materials will hold their shape and color much longer. When using metallic lures, scratch them up a little with a knife. The scratches will catch the sun's rays and send a glint of reflected light through the water into the path of a hungry fish.

> **Tight Lines**
> Scratch metallic lures with a small knife to catch the sun's rays and the attention of hungry fish with them.

Visual Hunting and Bait Variation

Certain colors are more visible than others in water, and this has obvious implications for the hunting habits of predatory species. Sharks are thought to prefer such colors, and the yellow associated with some lifejackets and kayaks is often referred to as "yum-yum yellow" by sailors and kayakers because, in addition to being highly noticeable by rescue teams, it is also thought to be highly visible and attractive to sharks. Although this hasn't been demonstrated conclusively, it makes sense and is supported by the apparent success of many yellow lures.

High visual contrast also increases visibility to sharks. Examples of this may include white soles of feet against the background of a tanned body or a black swimsuit against paler skin. In one instance, a shark apparently went after a

A selection of spoons and spinners illustrates how color, pattern, and, especially, shiny, reflective surfaces can be used to catch game fish.

swimmer's black tattoo, which stood out in high contrast against his skin. (Although some flesh came off with the tattoo, the swimmer survived.) Given the reflective surfaces of so many artificial lures, it should come as no surprise that shiny jewelry can attract predatory fish, including freshwater species. The only recorded pike attack on a person was evidently triggered by a diver's bright metallic watch.

An interesting observation was made in 1965 when two hundred topminnows were released into an aquarium containing twenty-four spotted piranhas. The observer watched as the piranhas chased the topminnows voraciously, and within an hour about a hundred had been eaten, with most of the remainder succumbing shortly thereafter. From the next day onward, the piranhas were fed meat, and twelve of the original two hundred topminnows remained alive and well. Perhaps these prey had survived long enough no longer to be seen as food by the piranhas, or perhaps they were simply so adept at evading predation that the piranhas deemed them uncatchable. When further topminnows were introduced, they were immediately hunted down and eaten, yet the original twelve remained unharmed. This provides strong evidence for the now well-known fact that fish are able to recognize other individuals and adapt their behavior accordingly. For anglers it provides a tip: if a fish is spooked by a plug or fly, it may recognize the same fly again and refuse to feed on it as a result. It is common for fish to follow a lure

Tight Lines
If a plug or fly is not producing results, it might be the result of nearby fish having been spooked by it. Try changing lures or location.

right back to the angler without taking the bait. When this happens regularly, it is time to change either your lure or your location.

Hearing

Though fish are perceived by humans as silent animals, this is far from the truth. Hitler's U-boats and the World War II arms race encouraged scientists to learn more about the dynamics of underwater sound, and much of our understanding of the subject and its influence on the lives of fish was established as a direct result of this research.

Research has found that fish are vocal animals, using low-frequency sounds to communicate during their day-to-day lives. Like birds, fish emit sounds when frightened, warning their school mates of danger. Fish advertise their presence with individually recognized social calls, and warning calls are shouted aggressively at their opponents.

The aquatic environment can be a noisy place, with rushing currents, vocalizing fish, footsteps on land, and the sound of rain at the water's surface. Furthermore, it's a highly variable environment, with changing light levels, degrees of turbidity, smells, and fluctuating volumes of sound. This has driven the evolution of a fish's complex sensory systems, including its sense of hearing, which provides a map of the world when other senses are unable to do so. Even in extremely turbid or turbulent conditions, a fish's sense of hearing enables it to locate prey and detect predators.

When we humans dive beneath the waves, water greatly reduces our hearing. This and the absence of visible external organs resembling our ears once led people to believe that fish were unable to hear. Karl von Frisch changed that in the 1930s with an experiment that involved blowing a whistle before feeding a blind bullhead. Von Frisch noticed that eventually the bullhead began to come out of its hole on hearing the whistle, in anticipation of food.

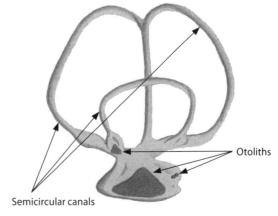

Otoliths

Semicircular canals

The inner ear of a fish.

The ears of fish have no external openings. Rather, the two inner ears are found close to the brain on either side of the fish's head. Each consists of three semi-circular canals containing fluid, and three chambers, each containing a hard ear bone, or *otolith*, that has a higher density than the surrounding tissue. This density difference causes the otoliths to quiver less than the rest of the fish's body as sound passes through it. Any movements of the otoliths are picked up by fine hairs lining the walls of the three chambers, which in turn send signals to the fish's brain.

As in humans, the ears of fish are used for balance as well as hearing. The fluid flows within the semicircular canals as the fish changes position. Further-more, otoliths are loose and act like simple gyroscopes. When a fish tilts to one side, they move relative to the surrounding tissue, enabling the fish to sense and correct its position in total darkness. The otoliths also lag behind as the fish accel-erates or overshoot as the fish suddenly stops, providing information to the fish about its speed. As previously noted, otoliths can be used to age fish as the inor-ganic salts making them are deposited faster at certain times than others, causing annual growth rings similar to those in trees.

Hearing alerts fish to the whereabouts of predators and prey. Sound waves provide information about the distance and direction of an object and even whether it is approaching or swimming away.

Since von Frisch's experiments, scientists have been testing the hearing of fish by rewarding them with food after particular sounds or combinations of sounds are played. If fish react to these sounds, they must be able to hear them. Such experi-ments have determined that most fish have good hearing and are particularly sensitive to low-pitch sounds in the range of 30 to 3,000 Hertz, or cycles per sec-ond. Salmonids are relatively limited—the upper end of their hearing range being around 1,500 Hertz unless the sound is particularly loud. Humans and other mam-mals are sensitive to a much larger frequency range than fish (20 to 20,000 Hertz), but fish are much better at pinpointing the direction of origin of a sound. People distinguish among sounds mostly on the basis of frequency, while fish key primar-ily on repetition rate and duration. Some fish, however, are able to heighten their sensitivity to a frequency of particular interest when exposed to high background noise levels, improving their ability to filter one call or sound from many others.

Sound Distance and Direction

The air above the surface of a lake is fourteen thousand times as compressible as the water below it, and this has major implications for how sound travels underwater. Oceanic fish have been known to return to their home territories on reefs after being displaced by as much as a kilometer. This return journey is thought to be navigated by the crashing sound of waves hitting the reef. The sounds made by boat propellers can travel many miles, and underwater explosions are clearly heard halfway around the world.

Sound underwater occurs in two forms: in particle displacement (motion of particles as sound passes through) and in pressure waves (waves of varying pressure emanating outward from the source). Sounds become quieter as they emanate from their source. Particle displacement is more important at close range, but pressure waves are more important farther away because only pressure waves carry over great distances.

Particle displacement causes a fish's otoliths to vibrate and is detected as sound. Pressure waves are picked up by the swim bladder, which, being filled with gas, is much more compressible than water or the fish's body. As pressure waves pass through the swim bladder, they cause it to change shape, resulting in particle displacement within the fish's body. In this way, fish are able to use their swim bladders to turn sound pressure into particle displacement, which is then detected by the otoliths. This use of the swim bladder increases the fish's sensitivity and the range of frequencies it is able to perceive. Amazingly, because of this, the hearing of certain fish can be aided by attaching a small balloon to the side of the head.

People use two strategies to determine the direction from which a sound emanates. First, we distinguish between the arrival times of the sound in each ear: even though the ears are separated by only a few inches, we can still tell if a sound arrives in one before the other, and that ear is obviously closer to the source of the sound. Second, our head blocks the sound from one side to a certain extent, so the ear that detects the higher volume is intuitively known to be closer to the source. (And the brain adjusts for different hearing ability in the two ears, so that a weaker ear closer to the sound is still perceived as being closer.)

Things are different for fish. Sound travels much faster through water than air, so the time lapse between ears is much shorter and harder to detect (Sound travels at 1,500 meters per second in water and only 300 meters per second in air.) Also, fishes' heads have much the same density as the surrounding water and therefore do not act as a sound break, and fishes' ears are (in most cases) closer together than our own. So how are fish able to determine what direction a sound is coming from?

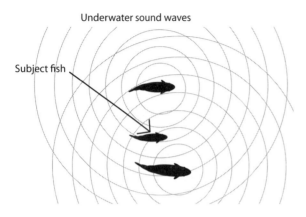

Underwater sound waves

Subject fish

Fish are able to detect the sound waves around them.

Fish rely entirely on the highly sensitive hairs within their ears. These are bent in accordance with the strength and frequency of any movements in the otoliths. This method is very effective. In fact, because of this three-dimensional system, fish maintain a real acoustic map of the positions of things around them. They can distinguish between sounds coming from various angles above, below, in front of, to the side of, or behind them much more accurately than people.

The Lateral Line

A fish also has an organ called the *lateral line*, which can detect sound and perform other sensory functions similar in some ways to hearing. Unlike its ears, the fish's lateral line can be clearly seen along the center of its flanks.

The lateral-line system consists of a series of pores arranged along a canal buried just beneath the fish's skin. (Pores connected to the lateral line are also present on the sides of the head.) The pores are open to the surrounding water, enabling it to flow in and out of the canal. Along the canal is a series of sensory cells that have

The lateral line of most fish is clearly visible along their flank.

fine hairs projecting from them. Any movement of water is detected by the hairs, which send signals to the brain. The hairs are sensitive to bending, and from this information, fish are able to detect in detail the water flow within their environment. (It is a little-known fact that many amphibians possess a lateral-line system as well.) The lateral line of a fish is highly sensitive, and care should be taken to avoid touching it when handling catch-and-release fish, as the pores can be destroyed easily. The lateral line develops as a fish grows—fish larvae have only a few pores compared with the well-developed system in adults.

Although the lateral line can in some circumstances pick up sound, the inner ear has a much greater sensitivity to sound and responds to a greater frequency range. The information available to a fish from its lateral line, however, can be just as important to its survival and to our understanding of the fish's behavior.

Imagine someone walking along a busy road. Even if the walker were stupid enough to close his eyes and plug his ears, he would still recognize the difference in air pressure between a passing bus and a passing car. In fish, this perception is much more refined.

Trout (particularly river-dwelling trout) spend a great deal of time hiding behind rocks waiting for food particles to be carried downstream to them by the current. In daylight, trout maintain their positions using vision, keeping in line with the landmarks around them. During the night, however, when the fish are unable to see, they use their lateral lines to sense the currents around them and thereby maintain position.

As fish swim, they leave vortices in the water similar to those left by boats. These disturbances linger as far as several meters behind fish and last several seconds. Fish can sense these with their lateral lines to detect the passing of another fish even after it is no longer visible. The trail of vortices may even be species-

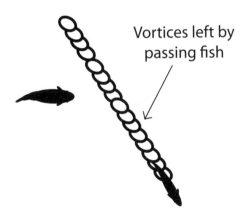

Vortices left by passing fish

Fish use their lateral lines to detect the movements of other fish by the vortices they leave as they swim.

The spinning spoon leaves a wake of vibrations that predatory fish are able to detect and will perhaps mistake for vortices left by a swimming prey species.

specific, and it is possible that some fish recognize other species by their vortex trails—an obvious benefit in finding prey or avoiding predation.

The sensitivity of a fish's lateral line depends both on the size of the fish and its speed through the water, so a large fish swimming at speed would get much more information about its environment than a small fish swimming slowly. The swimming motions of school fish may create enough turbulence to be detected several meters away, particularly if they are swimming at speed.

Fish are also able to perceive surface waves by means of their lateral lines. This enables them to feed on insects blown onto the water and trapped by its film. Some fish are able to block out frequencies associated with wind ripples and home in on the particular frequency created by an invertebrate in distress until the prey comes into sight. Dry-fly fishing might therefore be just as effective on a windy day as a flat calm.

> ### Tight Lines
> Dry-fly fishing might be as effective on windy days as it is during a flat calm.

The quivering exhibited by trout in their spawning behavior could be a way of stimulating the lateral line. The lateral line might be the organ through which trout and salmon feel sexual pleasure, ultimately triggering the release of eggs. This highlights how important the lateral line is as a sensory organ. Anglers who appreciate the sensitivity of the lateral line will try to make lure and fly movements that mimic as closely as is possible the movements of the prey they are imitating.

One theory currently suggested is that trout are able to use their lateral line for a primitive form of echolocation, similar to that used by dolphins. The theory is that trout pick up reflections of the waves they send out while moving through the water and use this information to gauge their surroundings. There is as yet no hard evidence for this, but such an ability would provide useful information about their environment, particularly at night.

Waves on the water's surface can be detected by fish below. When an angler's fly hits the surface, its waves attract fish.

Sound and Stalking

Many anglers will whisper to each other all day while banging their oars and feet on the bottom of the boat. This is exactly wrong. Airborne sounds such as voices are not much of a problem, as most of this noise is reflected away at the surface of the water. But impacts on solid objects in contact with the water are another matter. When a hydrophone is lowered into a pond, river, or lake, any footsteps around the edges are clearly heard. Likewise, any movement on a boat is clearly heard by fish some distance away. Keep footsteps and impact noises on the boat to a minimum. They will be heard by fish long before your speaking voice.

It's easy to see how lures designed to make a disturbance in the water, like spinners and poppers, can be used to attract fish by stimulating their lateral lines. It's highly likely that predatory fish interpret the vortices left by a spinner as the movements of a prey species. (The spinner also attracts attention visually through movement and reflection.) Other lures that use sound as an enticement incorporate beads that rattle or have solid surface features designed to create turbulence and vibrations.

When fish thrash about in distress, they produce low-frequency sounds. It has been shown that playing recordings of such sounds can attract predatory fish, especially in turbid or dark waters. Even the sounds made by the biting of prey food such as snails or shrimp have been found to excite hungry fish, and lures that re-create such sounds may be the next advance in fishing tackle.

Although we mentioned earlier that some fish can filter out background noises, this is only at lower noise levels. When environmental noise levels are high, however, fish have been found to become temporarily less sensitive to sound, much like people who are exposed to loud noises in a nightclub or at a construction site. Thus, when you fish in a rainstorm, in high winds that raise a chop on the surface, or in other noisy conditions, noisemaking lures will be less productive, and you should try highly visible lures instead. Visibility just below the surface will also be reduced in these conditions, but less so than audibility.

> **Tight Lines**
> Use high-visibility lures as opposed to noisemaking lures while fishing in a rainstorm or whenever noise conditions are a factor.

Smell and Taste

For generations fishermen have used chumming and ground-baiting methods to attract quarry, well aware of the powerful attraction that smell provides to a hungry fish. Smell plays a vital role in the day-to-day lives of fish. Like sound, it provides another mental map of their world even in total darkness, enabling them to locate school mates, predators, and food supplies. How does a freshwater fish's world smell and taste and how can this information help us to catch fish? Is there really any difference between smell and taste for fish?

The process by which fish sense the substances in their world is called *chemoreception*. It involves two separate sensory systems, olfaction (smell) and gustation (taste). It would be natural to assume that a fish uses its sense of smell for a long-distance search of its environment, allowing it to locate a food source. Once food is located, the fish could then use its sense of taste at close range to determine whether or not the food is edible. In reality, however, there is little difference between smell and taste for fish. Taste receptors have been shown to respond to chemical signals from distant sources. Although the systems responsible for smell and taste are physically separate in fish, they do more or less the same job.

Living on land and being surrounded by the air, people clearly differentiate between smell and taste. We associate smell with chemicals in the air and taste with chemicals that are dissolved in water (in our mouths). For the fish, however, all of the chemicals surrounding it are dissolved in water. Fish smell using their nostrils (*nares*). Taste occurs in the mouth, but fish also have taste buds situated elsewhere on their bodies, and, interestingly, a fish's taste buds are seldom found on their tongues, so it's probably reasonable to say that taste and smell overlap somewhat in the underwater world, with the difference between them being in the specific range of chemicals that the two systems are most sensitive to.

The Importance of Smell

The nasal cavities of a fish can be clearly seen on the top of its nose, in front of its eyes. There are two openings. The one at the front is the inlet into which water flows, and the one just behind it, nearest the eyes, is the outlet where water is released. Water passes through the nose as the fish swims. Unlike mammals' noses, fishes' noses are not connected to their mouths or respiratory systems.

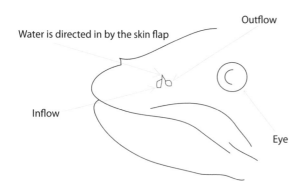

Water is directed in by the skin flap

Outflow

Inflow

Eye

The nostril of a rainbow trout.

Once the water enters the nose, it travels down the *inlet naris* (nostril) and reaches the *rosette*, where the actual smelling takes place. Scent molecules within the water come into contact with the thousands of receptor cells on the rosette, and signals are sent to the brain. After being smelled, the water and its entrained molecules are released via the outlet.

The rosette is the fish's organ of smell.

Unlike other sensory systems such as the ears, the fish's nose lacks a protective membrane and is in direct contact with the surrounding environment. For this reason, this sense is particularly vulnerable to pollutants (particularly heavy metals). There is good news, though: a fish's sense of smell can regenerate quickly when the source of the damage has been removed.

Interestingly, if a particular smell lingers within the water for any time, the fish's nose becomes desensitized to it, and the fish becomes less aware of its presence. Perhaps the regular use of modern scented baits within the same fishery could lead to a reduction in the attraction of resident fish to the baits' smell. This would only happen, of course, in a catch-and-release fishery.

The scent of food has an immediate effect on the behavior of hungry fish. Bottom-feeders begin foraging in the substrate. Surface-feeding fish begin to bite at anything that drifts past them. Fish seem to follow the same basic behavior pattern when following a scent trail. Once a scent has been picked up, fish become excited and begin to swim in the direction of the smell, gauging direction by sensing the varying intensity of the scent as the fish swims toward or away from it. If the scent trail is lost for any reason—while the fish hides from a passing bird, for example—a lake fish will begin to zigzag the area until it picks up the trail again. Fish swimming upstream in a river, however, will drift back downstream until the trail is picked up. Sharks are probably the fish that are best known for their ability to pick up and follow the scent of blood over great distances, but many other fish are equally sensitive. The European eel is able to detect the presence of a single molecule of alcohol within its nostrils.

Smell is perhaps more useful in enclosed freshwater spaces than in the open expanses of the sea. In lakes and rivers, smells stand a better chance of passing the nostrils of an inquisitive fish before they are dispersed.

Most freshwater fish prefer to feed during the daylight hours, particularly dawn and dusk, when light levels are balanced just right to provide safety from predators and the sun's glare while being light enough to see their prey. The species of fish that use smell as their primary sense to locate food are often nocturnal and tend to feed almost entirely on the bottoms of lakes or rivers. As mentioned earlier, the region of most freshwater fishes' brains devoted to smell is much smaller than that devoted to vision and considerably less developed.

Even among freshwater fish that are primarily visual predators, smell is vital in murky freshwaters to get within visual range of their prey. In the majority of cases, particularly in turbid water, smell provides the initial stimulus for the onset of a feeding response.

Salmon and sea trout are famous for having acute senses of smell. The life history of salmon and sea trout are well known. The young fish makes its journey downstream toward the sea, where it feeds voraciously in preparation for its return, when it will spawn in the waters from where it came. Migrating downstream to the sea is not thought to involve smell. The salmon simply follow the current. Once at sea, they are thought to use the position of the sun, the stars, and the earth's magnetic field to find their way around. It is only when they begin their return journey that their sense of smell comes into play. Blind salmon are able to return home almost as efficiently as those that could see. Salmon that are anosmic (cannot smell), however, consistently failed to return home.

It appears that salmon undergo a period of imprinting during which time they memorize for life the scent of their home river. What is it about their river to which they are attracted? There is evidence that they are responding to the specific smell of

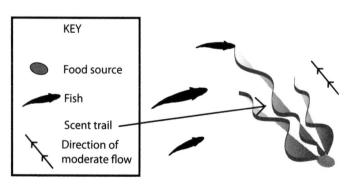

KEY

Food source

Fish

Scent trail

Direction of moderate flow

Flowing water creates a scent trail as it passes over the bait.

their own school mates. Different populations of fish release their own distinctive pheromones, and it is thought that the mucus on the skin of each fish may have its own individual smell, thus providing fish with a nonvisual way of identifying one another. The returning adults might follow the scent of their young freshwater relatives that have not yet traveled to sea.

When brown trout in a stream are lost due to a storm or a predatory attack, they are consistently able to find their way back to their home territories using their sense of smell. Just like salmon, trout with an intact sense of smell are able to find their way back from both upstream and downstream directions if displaced. Anosmic trout are unable to find their way back home, remaining instead in the same places they had been moved to, seemingly unable to sniff out their former homes. It seems that when a trout becomes lost, it follows a set of basic rules: if it can smell its home ground, then it swims upstream toward it, but if it cannot smell its territory, then it drifts downstream until it picks up the scent.

Olfaction is a fundamental player in sexual behavior, from the signaling of sexual status between individual fish to the discovery of and attraction to members of the opposite sex. Smell even drives the onset of maturity in young fish. These processes are governed by pheromones—chemicals released by fish (among other organisms) that affect the behavior of other individuals of the same species.

Carp exposed to wooden models of other carp ignored them, only becoming interested when the decoys were coated with mucus from other carp. Similar results have been found in salmonids. It seems, therefore, that coating a plug or lure with fish mucus could improve an angler's chances. Without such a coating or other artificial scent added, lures lack any scent likely to attract fish.

> **Tight Lines**
> Covering a plug or lure with fish mucus could improve an angler's chances.

Not all scents from a fish's own school mates are attractants, however. Von Frisch made an accidental discovery when one of his minnows was injured, and he noticed that other minnows within the aquarium began to flee. Certain species of fish possess large cells within their skin called *club cells*. These cells contain something aptly named *alarm substance*. The mucous cells that produce the fish's protective mucous membrane, familiar to all fishermen, secrete the mucus via a pore. The club cells, however, do not have a pore and are slightly deeper within the skin than the mucous cells, so the chemicals in them are only released when the skin is cut. A fish can even be killed, but as long as the skin is not cut, the alarm substance is not released. This is the fish's way of detecting the presence of a predator consuming its school mates in the weeds. The fright reaction is spread by a chemical stimulus, and fish dart for cover on smelling it.

Interestingly, in some circumstances, the alarm substance has been found to help the fish being attacked as well as their school mates. In addition to causing school mates to flee, it also attracts predators. Some predators, like pike, are highly competitive and may attack the fish who is in the midst of eating the one releasing the alarm substance. This can provide an opportunity for the victim to escape, injured but uneaten.

> **Tight Lines**
> Clean any tackle that might have come into contact with an alarm substance to avoid spooking other fish of the same species.

Research has shown that trout have club cells and possess the alarm response. Extracts of a school mate's skin in the water caused fear in juvenile rainbow trout. The same fear response was found in juvenile brown trout, but it is probably less important in adult fish that tend to spend more time alone.

This information is potentially very useful to anglers. Once a fish has been killed or cut, care should be taken to avoid transferring the alarm substance to tackle to avoid spooking other fish of the same species. Clean any tackle that might have come into contact with the alarm substance, and wash your hands after unhooking a fish and before handling your terminal tackle or rebaiting the hook.

It is worth mentioning that strong odors such as cigarettes or suntan lotion are rumored to put fish off their feed. I was unable to find any evidence that these odors repel fish, but they are unlikely attract them.

Taste and Appetite

Contrary to popular belief, fish do not necessarily eat every item of food that enters their mouth. Fish test their environment by tasting it, and many times a fish may simply be pecking at a baited hook to see if it is acceptable as food. (This, however, may be enough to get it caught.) After initially detecting the food and taking it into its mouth, a fish may well reject it if its taste is not acceptable.

As far as taste goes, trout are among the fussiest of the fishes. In experiments, a large number of fish species have been tested for their taste response to a variety of

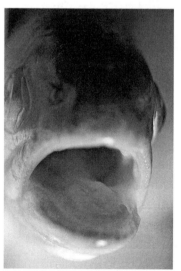

The last view of a trout's prey.

molecules. Most fish responded to a wide variety of stimuli, including the amino acid L-proline. Salmonids, however, responded very excitedly to L-proline and little else. The most sensitive tasters among the fish tested were catfish. (In fact, catfish have one of the most sensitive senses of taste of all vertebrates.) The fact that L-proline is so effective at stimulating the taste receptors of trout is hardly surprising, as it is one of the most common amino acids in invertebrate tissues. As many anglers know, it is possible to excite trout into biting by crushing and rubbing invertebrates onto a fly and moving it slowly. How legal this is depends on the fishery in question.

> **Tight Lines**
> When allowed (check individual fishery rules), it is possible to excite trout by crushing and rubbing invertebrates onto a fly and moving it slowly.

The larger the fish, the larger its meal, and the longer the fish will feed in order to satiate its appetite; an experiment carried out by J. M. Elliott in 1975 on brown trout found that meal duration was size-specific. In a controlled setting, trout weighing less than 100 grams required less than an hour to satisfy their appetites, while those weighing between 100 and 200 grams required up to two hours, and those weighing more than 200 grams fed for up to three hours. The feeding rate of the trout was found to be slightly slower at the beginning and at the end of the feeding period than in the middle.

A further paper by Elliott in the same year provided evidence that the number of meals consumed in a day depended on the quality of the food consumed. Trout feeding on mealworms, for example, took longer between mealtimes than those eating other, less rich prey items. He noted that the trout did feed occasionally between meals, but at much lower rates than those observed when the fish were actively feeding. In essence, fish snack between meals, but the best time to catch them is when they are actively feeding. This is normally at dawn and dusk.

Intelligence

The view that fish lack cognitive powers or even a basic memory is widespread. The reason for this is that the majority of people only see fish either on a market stall with faded colors and lifeless eyes or in a small goldfish bowl with nothing more than a plastic plant for inspiration. Even anglers can easily gain the wrong impression, for once they are pulled out of the water onto a boat or river bank, even wild fish can only flop about, appearing anything but intelligent. In tanks or on land, fish are not able to behave naturally and do not show the full and varied range of their behavior. The fact that they lack arms and hands capable of manipulating their environment does not help their cause. (It must be acknowledged, though, that dolphins and whales are recognized as intelligent creatures in spite of their fishlike bodies.)

Fish are seen to be lower on the "ladder of life" than other vertebrates, but this is not true. Fish, birds, and mammals all evolved during the Mesozoic period, approximately 170 million years ago. Contrary to popular belief, the evolutionary adaptation of fish did not stop when their offspring pulled themselves out of the water onto dry land; in fact, they have continued to adapt and spread into every habitat, becoming highly specialized in the process. Today there are more than twenty-five thousand species of fish surviving in almost every aquatic environment on earth. Each year approximately one hundred new species of fish are discovered to science.

Fish are highly evolved, socially aware creatures.

Over the past ten years, scientific research has focused on animal intelligence with some shocking findings. Recent studies have found that fish have abilities similar to nonhuman primates. They are able to interact with other individuals in highly complex social networks. They learn quickly and remember things for long periods of time. Certain species can live as long as humans, experiencing a great deal and learning from it. New research even credits fish with the human qualities of culture and empathy.

Sex and the Single Fish

In order to properly explore the cognitive abilities of fish, let's look at their behavior subject by subject. What better place to begin than sex?

Fish are extremely socially aware, one example of which is their courting behavior. In order to win a female, the males of many fish species fight one another. Studies have shown that when no females are watching, the males will end the fight as quickly as possible, not wasting energy or time once the winner is decided. When females are watching, however, the fights last longer and more injuries occur. Given an audience, the males will put on a show, the only purpose of which is to enhance their status in the eyes of another individual.

Fish are even able to recognize photographs of other fish and watch television! This ability has been exploited by scientists to test the fishes' interests. Researchers filmed a male performing a courtship dance to females. They then digitally erased the females so that the male appeared alone. The television was then placed next to a tank containing a female. While the male was feeding, the female did not show any interest, but as soon as he began his courtship dance, the female began watching the television and continued watching the whole time the male performed. Other researchers sped up the tapes and found that the females enjoyed the dance even more when it was played faster. From this research, it appears that females prefer more active males.

In another series of tests, scientists created dummies to represent female stickleback, then lowered them into a tank of males and watched as the males performed their courtship dances in front of the dummy females. They found that the males performed more vigorously in front of the females with the most distended bellies. (Interestingly, better-fed females also produce slightly larger eggs, indicating that the preference for the largest bellies may have a direct evolutionary advantage.) The males preferred females with impossibly outsized bellies to those females that had the largest naturally occurring bellies. This is an example of what fish biologists call a "supernormal stimulus," something familiar to many human males and a healthy source of earnings to many a Hollywood actress.

In similar experiments, female stickleback preferred the largest males. This behavior makes sense because larger males are better at defending their eggs and can expand their territories at the expense of smaller, weaker individuals.

Fish even have individual personalities. Highly aggressive male stickleback actually obtained fewer matings

Male stickleback may find this female's voluptuously swollen belly irresistible.

because they were always darting off to fight, even if it meant missing out on an already-eager female. It seems that some individuals prefer fighting to sex.

Eat or Be Eaten

As most fish are hunted by many other animals, they have evolved highly sophisticated methods of predator evasion. Fish are understandably very wary, and when faced with an unfamiliar fish species, they begin edging toward it, pausing at regular intervals to evaluate things from each slightly closer viewpoint. This behavior is called *predator approach* and is thought to be a method of assessing the level of threat the newcomer poses. The fish inspecting the newcomer are able to judge the relative safety of certain areas around the new fish, probably based on the position of the eyes, and seem to know that the most dangerous place to be is in the area directly in front of the predator.

Studies suggest that fish are able to recognize the facial features of predators. Those features causing the greatest intimidation in prey species are large eyes and, not surprisingly, a large mouth. When young trout are faced with a pike, they approach cautiously and then retreat back to the safety of the school. The nervousness of the whole school is expressed in the usual ways, moving jerkily and spending less time feeding. Interestingly, the fish that had approached the pike just prior to its attack appeared to be more stressed than the others, suggesting that prey fish are able to read the predator's body language and are aware of when it is about to attack.

The television-watching abilities of fish have been put to good use by salmon and trout farmers. They discovered that, because of hand-rearing, their fish were naive of predators, and as a result, large numbers of them were being killed within a few days of their release into the wild. An ingenious plan was put together to teach these fish the necessary life skills required in order to cope with predators before they were released. To do this, a few predator-experienced fish were introduced, followed by the scent of a predator. The naive fish watched as the experienced fish fled in fear. A television screen was lowered into their pens, and the fish were shown a film of predators along with the smell. The naive fish learned to react to the smell with a fear response even when the experienced fish had been removed. "Fish school" is an effective way of improving the life expectancy of hand-reared fish.

Fish are capable of great spatial awareness and can build up complex mental maps of their environment. Perhaps the best example of this is provided by the predator-escape response of the frillfin goby. These little fish live in coastal rock pools, and when the tide goes out, they become vulnerable to predators. They have evolved the ability to jump from pool to pool with pinpoint accuracy, missing the rocks in between. The fish are unable to see the surrounding pools while they are in the water, so this performance must be carried out entirely by memory. Scientists have found that when the tide is in, the gobies swim around and memorize the position of the local pools. They proved this by putting fish into previously unvisited rock pools and then encouraging them to jump. The fish, not having had time to explore the new territory, did not know where the nearest pools were and so refused to jump out of the water even when faced with serious danger.

Fish are forced to make complex risk assessments in their everyday lives. In schooling species such as rainbow trout, the fish that is leading the school will get to the best food first and ensure a plentiful supply for itself. This position is also the most dangerous, as the leader is the first to enter new territory and therefore the first to be grabbed by any predators lying in ambush. For territorial fish such as salmon or brown trout, the distance they will move to intercept passing prey items is reduced considerably when the fish are scared by the presence of a predator.

Feeding is a major part of the lives of all animals, not least fish, and one experiment shows how quickly fish can learn new skills in order to obtain food. Experimenters provided rainbow trout with a lever, which, when pressed, released food pellets into their tank. At first the fish would accidentally knock it, and the introduction of pellets meant that they eventually associated it with food. Interestingly, the fish then began to attack the lever itself as if it was food. This meant that when the pellets fell into the water, the fish were not in the right position to eat them before other fish swam up and stole them. As time passed, the fish learned to approach the lever slowly and lightly touch it while orienting themselves into the right position to intercept the pellets as they fell into the water. Within a few days, the fish were expertly handling the levers, and the scientists were even able to introduce levers of different colors, each providing a different food. They used this method to show that the trout preferred pellets flavored with fish to those flavored with mussels, a fact that will be of obvious interest to many anglers.

> **Tight Lines**
> Trout prefer the flavor of fish over the flavor of mussels.

Underwater Culture

As we have seen, recent experiments have put to rest the popularly held myth that fish have memories that last for only three seconds (it differs slightly by continent, but it's always a very small number). This belief seems to be based on the time it takes a fish to swim around its bowl. People seem to have assumed that because the fish starts swimming around again as soon as it's finished one lap, it must have forgotten the last one. The reality is that a fish in a goldfish bowl has little else to do, but given a natural, stimulating environment, fish clearly learn and remember for significant lengths of time.

Fish are very aware of the skills of their school mates and prefer to swim in schools with fish of equal foraging abilities, ensuring that all group members get adequate food. Perhaps not surprisingly, researchers have also shown that fish prefer to be around those that are good at spotting predators.

Aggressive fish have been found to use other individuals to make themselves "feel" better. When a trout is placed in a tank with a bigger fish and attacked by the larger individual, hormones are released making the smaller fish less assertive. If the bullied fish is then placed in a tank containing a fish smaller than itself, it will do more damage than normal as if to take out the frustration over its previous treatment on the smaller fish, reinstating itself as the dominant male. This behavior is known by scientists as *displacement aggression* and is common in animals and humans.

Perhaps the most interesting research yet undertaken provides insights into the personalities of fish. Individual fish show what is called *intraspecies personality*. This individuality among fish has been shown in experiments on stickleback, among others. These little fish are protective parents. Three-spined stickleback males are less likely to run from large predators such as rainbow trout if they are caring for eggs or young. Such parental care is vital, as the stickleback has poor adult survival rates. The protective behavior of fathers ensures that a high proportion of the eggs survive to leave the nest. Certain individuals are more aggressive than others, and this does not appear to be directly related to size. It seems that some individuals are simply braver than others. (Intriguingly, the determination of the father to stay with his young increased with both the number of offspring and their age.)

Furthermore, the young fish learn from their fathers and, as a result, stickleback reared by hand in the absence of a father show reduced predator-response behavior in later life. It seems that the fish learn how to respond to predators from their fathers during their first few days.

Fish are able to communicate with one another not just by making sounds but also by a complex array of subtle body language.

The latest research is even crediting fish with something that has been reserved in previous years for the most intelligent of all animals. Culture (the passing from one generation to the next of population-specific behavioral patterns) has previously been shown to exist in primates and aquatic mammals, but new research illustrates that fish pass on cultural traits just as humans do. Traditional migration routes, optimum feeding areas, mating grounds, and even resting sites are passed down from parent to young, one generation to the next. Such experiments have shown that fish would not be able to find the best grounds without this cultural transmission of information and that different populations of fish have different cultural tendencies.

Fish are also able to send signals to, and respond to signals from, different species. By recognizing the alarm calls or predator-evasion behavior of other species living within the same habitat, fish can hide at the first sign of danger. This behavior is also common in many birds that recognize the danger calls of others.

The past ten years have forced scientists to change the way they see fish. The next ten years are likely to shed even more light into their abilities and expose new capabilities that we currently only associate with "higher" mammals.

Fish are complex animals, capable of making behavioral decisions based on complex stimuli. Their entire lives are spent developing and adapting to environmental factors such as the weather, learning accordingly in the process. Next time you fail to catch, don't be too disappointed: if the latest science is anything to go by, fish are much smarter than anyone would have dared to suggest. This also means that the angler should make every effort to respect fish and take care to avoid unnecessary harm or suffering.

There is much more going on behind the eyes of a fish than many people think.

Fish Welfare

Stress can be a big problem for fish. Stress occurs when fish are exposed to environmental changes or circumstances such as excessive competition for food or capture by anglers. These situations cause fish to release stress hormones, which can severely weaken their immune systems, making them more prone to disease, and can even prove fatal. Of course, physical injury causes stress as well, and in many cases, it is impossible to clearly separate the harm done to a fish directly by a physical injury from the stress that it creates. In the following discussion of fishing practices, therefore, it may be taken as a given that any actions that minimize physical injury will also minimize stress and so play a double role in contributing to the fish's survival.

The Price of Freedom

In any catch-and-release fishery, it is important to keep stress to a minimum to maximize the fish's chances of survival. Well-cared-for fish will survive and grow, to be caught again when they are even bigger and stronger. Badly handled fish are likely to become overstressed and die. The average recovery time for rod-caught fish that were handled carefully and for a minimum time is around twelve hours. During this time, the fish rest on the bottom, after which they resume feeding. Fish returned to the water alive do not always recover, however. If they have been exposed for too long, they are likely to sink to the bottom and die.

Air Temperature

> *Tight Lines*
> Fish being returned to the water should be put back as soon as possible.

The temperature of the air influences the survival times (the period of time that fish are able to survive out of the water) of fish that have been removed from the water as well. One study found that trout from fish farms removed from the water and exposed to the air died significantly faster at higher air temperatures. This is of particular relevance to anglers when fishing in warm weather. In all cases, fish being returned to the water should be put back as soon as possible.

Hooks

Hooks come in various sizes, with and without barbs. Generally, fish caught on smaller hooks come to less harm than those caught on larger hooks. It is also worth noting that a bait or fly presented on a smaller hook will in many cases be more attractive to fish and so increase the angler's chances of hooking up in the first place.

Barbless hooks should be used wherever possible. Barbs can cause unnecessary damage to fish during hook removal, and barbless hooks will hold fish perfectly well providing the line is kept taut at all times. Treble hooks, too, should be avoided, because on hookup, two of the three hooks often remain unembedded. As the fish fights, the hook pivots around the one embedded hook, and the unembedded hooks can come into contact with the fish's skin and eyes, causing severe injuries.

> **Tight Lines**
> A bait or fly presented on a smaller hook will in many cases be more attractive to fish.

Barbed and barbless hooks.

Anglers themselves can also get injured when using trebles. If the fish thrashes around during unhooking, the loose hooks can easily get embedded in an angler's finger. Many modern plugs come with single hooks. These catch fish just as effectively as trebles.

Removing a fish from the water can be extremely stressful, so it is best to unhook the fish while it is still in the water. When using barbless hooks, it is often possible to unhook a fish without even touching it: grip the shank of the hook with your fingers, and it should come out easily. If the fish is exhausted (it may roll onto its side or back), then cradle the fish in the palm of your hand below the water (taking care not to touch the lateral lines). In moving water, face the fish into the current; this will allow it to catch its breath, and usually within a few seconds, it will swim away. If it is necessary to remove the fish from the water, first wet and cool your hands in the water. Avoid touching the sensitive areas of the fish's body—the eyes, gills,

Avoid treble hooks like the ones on this large (12-centimeter) lure. They don't significantly increase hookups, but they can easily injure fish.

and lateral line. Many fish are unable to close their eyes, so to protect their eyes, never place them on hard ground or in the bottom of a boat to flap around for even a few seconds. All this will help prevent damaging and stressing the fish.

Net Mesh and Lines

Modern net mesh is designed to be less abrasive than some older nets. It is worth replacing your nets if they are getting rough to touch. Smooth, soft nets will not scratch the fish's eyes or flanks.

Tight Lines
Stronger line improves your chances of catching fish while ensuring that they don't swim away with a hook in their mouth.

Make sure the line you are using is the correct weight for your target species. Line that is too light is likely to break, leaving the fish with a hook possibly embedded in its mouth and a length of line trailing. At best, this could interfere with its feeding, and at worst, it could get tangled on a snag, resulting in an unnecessary death. Stronger line will increase your chances of catching the fish, decrease your chances of losing your terminal tackle, and ensure that the fish is returned to the water without a hook left in its mouth.

Many anglers believe that using lighter line is more sporting. I would argue that the skill involved in angling comes from knowing how to tie a strong knot, when to release line, and when to apply pressure and pull the fish in. More fish are lost when pressure is applied at the wrong moment and the hook comes free than when the line breaks. For this reason, fishing with stronger line in no way reduces the sporting skill required to bring the fish in. The only difference is that when a fish outwits the angler and loses the hook, it can return safely to its home waters to fight another day. In a line-break situation, the fish is likely to be impaired for the rest of its life. Choosing line strength is a matter of responsible angling and having respect for your quarry. If a fish is smart enough to outwit you, then it should be free.

Always dispose of line and hooks carefully. Line should be wrapped around your fingers and then cut into one-inch sections. Fishing line can cause severe damage to fish and other wildlife if left in the field. Hooks should be taken home and disposed of safely. Under no circumstances should a baited hook be left by the water. The bait will attract more than just fish, and any animal that consumes it is likely to be seriously harmed.

Gut-Hooking and Foul-Hooking

"Gut-hooking" is what happens when a fish swallows the bait deeply and gets hooked in the stomach. Even with unhooking tools, it can then be difficult to remove the hook, and it will significantly increase the stress caused to the fish. Gut-hooking can and should be avoided by following a few rules:

▶ Keep in touch with your bait. If your method of fishing allows, make sure that the line between your rod tip and hook is tight at all times. This can be impracticable when fly- or bobber-fishing, but it is good practice with techniques such as trolling, bottom-fishing, and spin-casting, enabling you to detect even tiny knocks on the hook and leading to more hookups, while reducing the chances of gut-hooking.

▶ Try to strike as soon as the fish takes the bait and do not wait until the fish has had time to swallow it. You may miss a few hookups, but this is a sacrifice worth making to ensure that the fish do not come to unnecessary harm.

▶ Prepare the bait so that the point of the hook is visible. This will increase the chances of hooking the fish and will make the fish less likely to swallow the bait.

▶ When practical, fish flies and lures, as they are less likely to be swallowed whole than large baits. Fish will snap at these artificial lures and quickly realize they are inedible. In most cases, this initial snap is all that is needed for the hook to set.

"Foul-hooking" occurs when a fish is hooked on a fin or in its flank. A slower retrieve is less likely to foul-hook a fish, but sometimes fast retrieves are necessary, and foul-hooking can occur in spite of an angler's best intentions. In most cases, it is easy to tell that a fish is foul-hooked. It will seem to weigh more than expected, and you will not feel the characteristic side-to-side knocking that occurs when a fish shakes its head in an attempt to free the hook. In some cases, though, you only notice the foul-hooking when the fish is brought to the surface.

If you suspect you have foul-hooked a fish, play it softly. Give the fish plenty of line, while being careful not to allow it to snag the line on any underwater obstructions. Instead of putting pressure on the fish to bring it in, allow the fish to tire itself out by swimming. The less pressure you put on the line, the less damage the hook will do. Once the fish has tired, bring it into the landing net and carefully remove the hook. The fish can then be cradled and released.

If a fish is badly gut-hooked or foul-hooked, it may be more humane to knock it on the head and end its suffering, although if you are able to remove the hook without causing too much damage, then returning the fish alive is the best course of action.

CHAPTER 2

Where the Fish Are Through the Day

Environmental changes occur over different periods of time. While some weather changes take a whole season to occur, every angler knows all too well that others can occur in a matter of minutes. This chapter covers those changes that can occur over relatively short periods of time. Any sudden change in the weather can cause an equally sudden change in the behavior of fish, and understanding the implications of these changes will give the angler the ability to adjust his or her fishing tactics according to the weather of the moment.

Research highlights an important point: fish change their behavior not only in response to changes in single environmental variables, but also in response to numerous variables changing simultaneously. An experiment was designed to discover the effect a gradient in light intensity would have on the choices made by lake whitefish when they were presented with other "competing gradients." The scientists noted that the presence of numerous choices between competing variables led the fish to make compromises. Fish normally avoid water containing the toxin cadmium, preferring cadmium-free water. They also prefer subdued light to bright light. A special aquarium was set up, in which levels of cadmium and light intensity could be independently controlled and changed from one end to the other. When given a choice, the fish preferred to stay in the water containing cadmium rather than swim in the side of the aquarium with the highest light intensity. As soon as the lights were turned off, equalizing the light intensity across the aquarium, the fish swam into the cadmium-free water. Similar experiments have shown that brook char prefer optimum temperature regions over areas where light levels are optimum, even choosing to remain in areas with light levels they would normally avoid so long as the temperature was preferred. Walleye have been shown to select light intensities over oxygen levels. In all of these experiments, the fish remain in the preferred region of their preferred weather variable as the gradients are increased, getting more and more uncomfortable until eventually, at a critical level, they abandon their initial instincts and move away. This point is not reached until levels have risen significantly higher than those avoided by fish when all other factors are equal.

Light

It is light, working through the process of natural selection, that has determined the outward appearance of fish. They have evolved patterns and colors to communicate to one another and to camouflage themselves against the habitats in which they live. It is said that there is not a color known to man that is not represented on the body of a fish somewhere in the world. (This is perhaps not surprising, given that there are more than twenty-five thousand species of fish living on earth.)

Light properties within water are dramatically affected by both local and general meteorological conditions. The light intensity near the surface varies considerably over the course of a day, most rapidly during the twilight periods of dawn and dusk. Light intensity in surface waters changes by 0.1 percent per minute at midday and by as much as 50 percent per minute at dawn and dusk. Clouds suddenly moving over the sun can reduce light intensity by up to 75 percent within a few seconds.

These changes, though rapid, are almost nothing compared to the changes in light intensity that occur when a wave passes over the surface. Surface waves can change the light intensity by as much as 200 percent per second. Local surface disturbances caused by wind-driven ripples and waves act as lenses, changing the light intensity at a given point below the surface. In bright sunlight, the effect of the waves can be easily seen as the light flickers along an underwater object such as the back of a fish or the lake bed. This flickering can momentarily enhance the visual contrast of objects, making them easier for fish to spot.

Day length follows the seasons in general, but the amount and rate of change vary with latitude. Close to the equator, the duration of darkness and daylight changes by only several minutes from season to season. In the middle latitudes, day and night vary seasonally by several hours. In the highest latitudes, above the

Arctic and Antarctic circles, days can last twenty-four hours in summer, and nights twenty-four hours in winter.

Likewise, the *rate* of change in diurnal light intensity is greater at lower latitudes and less significant at higher latitudes. In other words, darkness falls and dawn breaks more abruptly in the tropics, and more gradually near the poles. Fish that live in the tropics therefore experience minor changes in total amount of daylight from season to season but rapid changes in light levels on a daily basis, while the opposite is true for those living in high latitudes (fish in the temperate zones experience something between the two). The greater seasonal changes of the higher latitudes have been more significant than the greater daily changes of the lower latitudes in producing specific adaptations in the behavior of fish.

Day and Night

Nocturnal animals are active during the night, and diurnal animals are active during the hours of daylight. Fish populations tend to be either nocturnal or diurnal, but many species of both categories are particularly active during the twilight periods of dawn and dusk. Species that are particularly active during these twilight times are said to be *crepuscular.*

Many fish are *crepuscular*—that is, particularly active during the twilight periods of dawn and dusk.

An interesting phenomenon can be observed on coral reefs. For a period of about twenty minutes both just after sunset and just before dawn, both the diurnal and nocturnal fish hide among the cracks in the reef. The reason for this so-called quiet period is that neither the cones (the parts of the eye primarily used by diurnal fishes) nor the rods (the parts of the eye primarily used by nocturnal fishes) work at their best during this period of intermediate light levels. This fact is well known by numerous species of reef predators, who would, if these prey fish remained active and out in the open, take advantage of their prey's lessened ability to notice their stalking behavior. The prey fish return to the open water of the reef only when their eyes have become adjusted to the changing light levels and they are less vulnerable to the predators.

> ***Tight Lines***
> An interesting phenomenon can be observed on coral reefs. For a period of about twenty minutes both just after sunset and just before dawn, both the diurnal and nocturnal fish hide among the cracks in the reef.

Predator avoidance is just one of many fish behaviors that are influenced by daily changes in light. Another was shown in an experiment with rainbow trout that provides a glimpse into the influence light has on their feeding behavior. Trout were placed in tanks, each of which was equipped with a "demand feeder" that dispensed 1 gram of food each time a stainless steel level was activated by the fish. The lever was placed 2 centimeters above the surface of the water to prevent its accidental operation. (When the lever was placed below the water surface, the amount of food wastage left at the bottom of the tanks increased greatly, indicating that the lever was being triggered accidentally by fish bumping into it.) As the tanks were indoors, daylight was controlled artificially. Using a dimmer, 30 minutes of artificial dawn and dusk were created at the beginning and end of each artificial day. A large increase in feeding activity was observed at dawn followed by a smaller increase at dusk. Just under 50 percent of the total daily feeding activity occurred during the first four hours of daylight.

Interestingly (as previously discussed), the scientists conducting the study noted that rainbow trout appeared to have "meals" where feeding activity occurred in short bursts. The presence of food and the act of feeding itself caused a feedback effect, encouraging the fish to feed. This is in contrast to other fish such as the carp family that are agastric (lacking a stomach). Carp graze constantly, feeding little and often.

Further interesting observations were made during the experiment concerning other aspects of trout behavior, including the species' ability to learn. The lever was always activated by the dominant fish. There were no unusual growth patterns, so all fish had access to food. It was suggested that although the dominant fish was always responsible for the activation of the lever, the whole shoal began feeding as soon as the food entered the water. In this way, the dominant fish initiated feeding periods within the shoal. The scientists also observed that two meals a day promoted maximum growth. One daily meal caused reduced growth, and three meals per day did not improve growth rates.

As the sun sweeps across the sky, the angle of sunlight changes in relation to any given body of water. Sections of rivers and streams flowing toward the sun at any given moment therefore provide different light conditions than sections flowing away from it. Given that most fish display the behavior known as *rheotaxis*—that is, a preference to face into the current (see Chapter 1)—it is likely that fish in sections of river in which the current is flowing *away from* the sun (for example, west-flowing rivers in early morning) could be temporarily blinded by its glare on bright days. Under these conditions, the fish's abilities to find food and detect predators are both reduced, and it is also likely, as a result, that the fish will spend this time hiding and conserving energy. As the sun moves overhead and behind the fish, the visual conditions for feeding are likely to improve; the fish will come out of hiding and begin looking for a meal, and that is an advantageous time to go fishing. It is important to note that this scenario is only likely to make a significant difference on particularly bright days and in clear, shallow water.

In the winter months, trout select habitats with different water velocities and substrate features during daylight from those during darkness, based on their feeding and predator-avoidance habits. In winter, riverine trout prefer to feed at night in order to avoid visual hunters, such as mammals. (Interestingly, the lower temperatures of nighttime cause physiological changes within the fishes' eyes that improve their night vision.) During the daytime, they hide behind rocks and other submerged features and prefer a coarse substrate (river bottom) that protects them from the flow. Since they place themselves outside of the current's main flow and additionally wedge themselves in place as a further aid to remaining stationary, a rapid current is not much of a liability, and in practice, a trout's winter daytime habitats are often characterized by higher water velocity than those they seek at night.

> **Tight Lines**
> As the sun moves overhead and behind the fish, the fish will come out of hiding and begin looking for a meal, and that is an advantageous time to go fishing.

Tight Lines
River-dwelling trout
are likely to be found
feeding over finer
gravels in slower water
at night and sheltering
from the flow behind
larger rocks in faster
water during the day.

When trout hunt at night, they must place themselves in a better position to catch a meal. This means exposing themselves to the current, so naturally they prefer areas of lower current velocity in order to conserve energy. This is particularly important in cold weather. To sum up: river-dwelling trout are likely to be found feeding over finer gravels in slower water at night and sheltering from the flow behind larger rocks in faster water during the day.

One study of the activity of stream-dwelling adult brown trout began with twenty-nine fish caught with a rod and line and then released after a transmitter was implanted into each. Recording their movements, it was observed that the trout were nocturnal, moving over greater distances and being generally more active during the hours of twilight and night than by day. They were also noted to be active for eleven hours per day, with activity beginning as soon as the sun set and continuing through the night. Activity ceased at sunrise, and the fish remained relatively inactive during the hours of daylight.

Individual trout patrolled the same areas every day. Each fish was likely to be found in the same location at the beginning and end of each twenty-four-hour period. Large river-dwelling trout have a routine! In the study, they moved an average of 121 meters per day and maintained an average home range of 41 meters. These findings highlight the territoriality of brown trout. Larger trout moved over greater distances and defended larger territories than smaller ones. The study suggested that this was the result of the larger fishes' greater energy requirements, necessitating a larger foraging area. For the angler, this information has obvious applications. Creatures of habit are easier to locate regularly once they have been seen in the first instance.

The behavior of certain species of fish, including trout, of keeping their fins in contact with the bed of the

Fish do not hunt by sight at night, so choose a bait or lure that attracts fish by smell or sound.

stream is thought to help with orientation in the absence of light. This is a useful fact for anglers. When fishing for trout at night, present a bait that can be found without the aid of vision on the stream, lake, or river bed. These include heavily scented baits such as slugs, snails, dead fish, or meats.

Dawn and dusk are particularly good feeding, and therefore fishing, times for most species. The activity levels of both nocturnal and diurnal species peak at these times. The changing light levels indicate to the fish that their day is about to begin or end. If the fish's day is just beginning, it is hungry after a long period of not eating, and its feeding activity will be at its peak. If its day is ending, it will feed to prepare for the long rest period ahead. For these reasons, dawn seems to be better for daylight-feeding fish, and dusk seems to be better for nocturnal species. As previously mentioned, though, there are frequent exceptions to this general rule.

> **Tight Lines**
> The activity levels of both nocturnal and diurnal species peak at dawn and again at dusk, making both particularly good feeding times, and therefore good fishing times for most species.

Dawn is the most productive time to fish for most daylight-feeding fish.

Dusk and Dawn

Many schooling species break up at night. This is thought to be due to the reduced risk of predation and therefore the reduced need for safety in numbers. The scientist F. R. Harden Jones observed some interesting changes in fish behavior with falling light levels. While observing European minnows, he noticed that the school would begin to loosen as light intensity was reduced. Below a critical light intensity, the school would break up. This critical level was described by Harden Jones as being just below the intensity of moonlight. A further decrease in light intensity induced a period of heightened activity, during which the minnows frequently broke the surface of the water. This behavior came to an end after a few minutes. Following this activity, the light was turned on again, and the fish were seen to be resting, scattered individually on the bottom of the tank. Perhaps this behavior can be compared to the excitement of roosting birds before they settle for the night.

Scientific analysis of shark attacks on humans have shown that they peak twice a day, once at about 11 A.M. and again at about 4 P.M., with the afternoon being more dangerous than the morning peak. This highlights an overlap period between fishes' feeding habits at dusk and dawn and the times when people are in the water. (Sharks probably feed earlier and later than these times—just not on people, as we tend not to be swimming much outside the eleven-to-four window.)

As popularized in the film *Jaws*, in 1945, less than a month before the end of World War II, the heavy cruiser USS *Indianapolis* was torpedoed by a Japanese submarine in the Philippine Sea and sank in a matter of minutes. Survivors of the explosion entered the water, where sharks quickly surrounded and killed a large number of them. Due to errors of communication, rescue was delayed several days, during which time the men continued to float in the warm water and attempt to fend off shark attacks. Those who were finally rescued (only a quarter of the twelve-hundred-man crew) noted that late evening was the most dangerous time and that the feeding and screaming went on throughout the nights.

At night, sharks have an increased sensory advantage over us. (Their advantage is big enough during daylight, of course.) Sharks attack their prey from below, because from this angle, the prey's silhouette is at its clearest, and it has fewer escape routes. At the same time, our ability to see them below us in the water is less than during daylight periods.

Moonlight and Tides

Why are so many animals directly influenced by the lunar cycle? Billions of years ago, life on earth was influenced by a lunar gravitational force one thousand times more powerful than today. As the earth's spin began to slow down, the moon began to drift farther away. But while the effect of the moon's gravity, per se, on animal behavior remains a subject of scientific dispute, the moon still maintains its evolutionary grip.

During solar eclipses, daylight is temporarily blocked out by the moon. Although this dark phase, called *totality*, lasts for only a few minutes, it is long enough to influence the behavior of many animals, including fish. During a solar eclipse on August 11, 1999, I was lucky enough to be on the banks of a large reservoir. As darkness fell,

I saw fish rising avidly, as they do at sundown. It appears that the decline in the light intensity tricked the fish into thinking that it was dusk. A few bats even appeared, showing how quickly animals react to changing environmental conditions.

Many diurnal fish feed at night around the period of the full moon, as the extra light increases both insect activity and the fishes' visual capabilities. On the day following a full moon, these fish tend to be well fed and will rest rather than feed. During a full moon, the light is intense enough to cast shadows on the water, and if you approach the water with the moon at your back, you will likely scare off surface-feeding fish.

> *Tight Lines*
> Many diurnal fish feed at night around the period of the full moon, as the extra light increases both insect activity and the fishes' visual capabilities.

The days when the fish will feed most actively are likely to be those between the last quarter and the new moon when extreme darkness during the previous night has inhibited feeding.

There are ways an angler can combine knowledge of light and the tides to his or her advantage. For example, plankton live in vast quantities in large freshwater lakes and in the sea, particularly near shore areas, where nutrient levels are highest. They move up and down within the water column to remain in their optimum light conditions. At night, they rise higher, and as the sun appears, they sink back down. At sea, when the rising tide coincides with the upward migration, organisms are washed ashore in abundance. When the rising tide coincides with the downward migration, however, then fewer organisms will be washed ashore.

The level at which plankton are situated during flood tide has a real influence on coastal fish. The plankton are too small to imitate as bait, but they attract small fish, which in turn attract larger ones of interest to anglers. The best tides to fish are therefore incoming, or flood, tides that occur at the darkest times of the month, when the plankton are at their highest within the water column.

Daily Oxygen Variables

Just as people suffer quickly in a reduced-oxygen environment, so do fish. Habitats with low levels of oxygen cause fish to move quickly away. An early experiment provides valuable insight into just how aggressively fish react to reduced oxygen levels. Two streams of water were put together in such a way that the fish being observed could pass freely between them. The setup allowed the experimenter to manipulate the oxygen concentrations in each of the streams independently and observe the fishes' behavior. Observing the behavior of freshwater stickleback, minnows, and trout fry, it was found that when the fish entered the stream with comparatively low levels of dissolved oxygen, their respiratory movements increased significantly. This behavior was followed by random movements and violent struggling. The fish were sometimes so disoriented that they swam on their sides. Their thrashing and undirected movements eventually resulted in them

randomly finding their way into the well-oxygenated stream. As soon as the fish entered the oxygen-rich side, their rapid convulsions ceased, and they rested on the bottom of the tank while their gill movements quickly returned to normal. The reaction of the fish was thought to be a behavioral response to water of dangerously low oxygen concentration. The instinctive behavior of stopping all movement as soon as their oxygen requirements were met prevented the fish from accidentally reentering the oxygen-poor area and

Oxygen dissolved in water is usually the most immediately important environmental factor affecting fish.

ensured an adequate supply of oxygen. Further, the violent movements observed during exposure to low oxygen levels could be a way of maintaining maximum oxygen uptake, since rapid movement results in more water passing over the gills and so aids in respiration.

The experiment was repeated at lower temperatures, and the same behavior was observed, but at a reduced speed. When the temperature was increased, the fish developed distress very rapidly and turned back before they had fully entered the poorly oxygenated water. Only fish swimming rapidly entered the stream of low oxygen concentration; distress followed quickly, and their spasms returned them to the safety of the high-oxygen stream. Interestingly, the minnows were found to be much faster than the stickleback when

Tight Lines
Fish will not remain in poorly oxygenated water. Avoid fishing in areas where pollution has temporarily but significantly reduced oxygen levels.

swimming from the poorly oxygenated water into the well-oxygenated water. The trout fry would often enter the oxygen boundary, gulp, stagger, and then return to well-oxygenated water. For the angler, this behavior indicates that fish will not remain in poorly oxygenated water. Avoid fishing in areas where pollution has temporarily but significantly reduced oxygen levels.

Oxygenating Plants

Plants produce and consume oxygen at different times of day. During daylight hours, plants produce energy using the sun's light via the process of photosynthesis. This process involves the production of oxygen. When the sun is shining, all of the plants within a body of water are releasing oxygen. At night, the plants cannot use the sun's light, so they respire, taking in oxygen from the surrounding water. This means that

Plants provide fish with oxygen, cover, and food.

oxygen levels in the water are at their daily lowest at dawn, as the plants have been using up oxygen all night. At dusk, oxygen levels are at their highest, as the plants have been releasing oxygen into the water all day. This effect is more relevant to enclosed bodies of water where flow does not have a mixing effect, which tends to oxygenate water. It is also somewhat localized within a given pond or lake, with proximity to large amounts of vegetation having a marked effect on the immediate levels of dissolved oxygen.

Two related factors concerning aquatic plants must be borne in mind when considering the effects of daily oxygen variation on fishes' behavior:

▶ Plants provide cover from predators. During the day, this is especially important, as most predators hunt

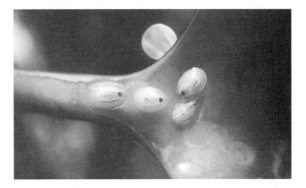

Plants harbor a vast variety of food sources for fish, including insects, crustaceans, mollusks, and young fish. These blue-rayed limpets are attached to a kelp frond.

using sight. At night, when they are less exposed to predators hunting by sight, cover is less important to prey fish.

▶ Plants are a good source of food for fish, both the vegetation itself and the myriad of invertebrates that live among the leaves. For this reason, fish can often be found foraging in and around weed beds. But fish also enjoy taking advantage of food items in more exposed areas of water, and they choose optimum times for doing both, balancing the risk of being eaten against the benefit of finding food.

Effects of Temperature on Oxygenation and Oxygen Use

Most species of fish feed mainly at dawn and dusk. At dawn, oxygen levels are low around any vegetation. The temperature will also be comparatively low after the long night. Generally speaking, the higher the oxygen, the higher the fishes' activity levels are.

Fish prefer lower temperatures when oxygen in the water is reduced. This is because chemical reactions take longer at lower temperatures, so blood oxygen lasts longer. Lower temperatures also increase the affinity of their blood to oxygen. Additionally, cold water can hold more dissolved oxygen than warm water. By selecting areas of low temperature during periods of oxygen shortage, fish increase the amount of time they are able to survive. Once daylight returns and the plants have brought oxygen levels back up in the lake, fish seek out feeding grounds in warmer water again.

> **Tight Lines**
> When oxygen levels are low, as at dawn, fish seek deeper areas of low flow with little or no weed.

Low oxygen levels can be best tolerated when they are relatively constant, but rapid changes in oxygen levels are particularly stressful to fish, as demonstrated by the previously described oxygen level experiments. For this reason, when oxygen levels are low, as at dawn, fish seek areas of relatively constant oxygen levels. These include deeper areas of low flow with little or no weed.

Fish feed slowly in these areas because of both the colder temperatures and the low oxygen levels. Feeding in these areas is believed to be short-lived, however, for when the light gets bright, the fish will seek cover from predators.

At dusk, when oxygen levels are at their highest, fish will tend to feed deep within the weed beds. As the sun has been shining all day and the water is warm, the fish will have more energy and are more likely to feed actively both at the surface and in deeper water. Fish are also more inclined to travel for food at dusk, so surface fishing at this time can be very productive. As the light fades, the fish will feed increasingly closer to the surface as the risk from predation decreases.

In contrast, fish are more inclined to resist traveling at dawn, so fly fishermen will do well to use a small nymph, moved slowly around the edges of a weed bed or in open water. Cast deep and regularly: the key here is to cover plenty of water to find out where the fish are gathered and feeding. Within any given fishery, this is likely to be the same location, day after day, so always seek the advice of local anglers. At dusk, the fly fisherman would be better served by a dry fly dropped right onto the edge of a reed bed in the margins. It is important to note here that the impact of plants and oxygen is only likely to influence fish significantly in relatively small still waters or larger waters that are densely weeded throughout.

Many fish lurk around plants, seeking both forage food and cover from predators.

(a) When fishing at dawn, use weighted fly patterns to fish deep. (b) When fishing at dusk, fish buoyant surface water flies close to reed beds or margins.

Temperature Variation and Its Influence on Behavior

Air cools down and heats up much more quickly than water. For this reason, the aquatic environment can be seen as a temperature buffer protecting the animals living within it. As mentioned earlier, significant changes in water temperature occur more commonly and more rapidly in shallow fresh water than in the deep seas because it takes less time to heat or cool a smaller volume of water.

Within any body of water, temperatures rise and fall both daily and seasonally, driven by water currents and the surface weather. Cloud cover influences the rate at which surface waters heat and cool in reaction to the surrounding temperature. During the day, of course, cloud cover will reduce the amount of solar radiation reaching and heating the water. After sunset, however, the opposite effect occurs: clouds reflect the radiant heat emanating from the water and the surrounding ground back onto earth and water, delaying the cooling process.

The sun will rapidly warm a shallow stream, especially one with a dark bottom.

Because surface waters absorb so much sunlight, converting it to heat, deeper waters naturally remain cooler. In very shallow water, the color of the river or lake bed plays a role. A dark-colored bed will absorb the sun's heat and heat the water above it, while a light-colored bed will reflect the heat back. The hot and cold patches can influence fishes' location and behavior.

Water temperatures usually lag behind the seasons by a few weeks when compared to conditions on land. Water in lakes, ponds, and streams reaches its warmest temperatures a few weeks after summer's hottest air temperatures and is at its coldest around the time that the air has begun warming up.

These temperature changes have profound effects on the behavior of fish. A study of the amount of time that trout required to digest food used a small pump to empty the stomachs of trout at varying times after they had eaten a known amount of food, and then weighed the contents (it was noted that the pump did not appear to affect the trout and that the fish recovered rapidly when returned to their tank). The experiment was performed at different temperatures, with the effects on digestion recorded for each variation. The results showed that as the water temperature increased, so did the speed of digestion.

Years later, the study was expanded, and it was found that the appetite of brown trout varied with temperature. Between 38.84°F (3.8°C) and 55.94°F (13.3°C), the size of the meals eaten increased significantly. Between 55.94°F (13.3°C) and 65.12°F (18.4°C), meal sizes increased slightly. And between 65.12°F (18.4°C) and 70.88°F (21.6°C), the rate of feeding decreased rapidly.

Other aspects of behavior also varied with temperature. Below 42.8°F (6°C), the trout were inactive and reluctant to feed, while above 66.2°F (19°C), they were active but refused to feed.

It was further learned that maximum growth occurred at 64.4°F (18°C) when the fish were able to feed until they were satisfied three times a day. If the number of meals were reduced to two, then maximum growth would occur at 55.40°F (13°C).

Different species of fish prefer different optimum temperatures within different temperature ranges. In the following table, the temperatures represent the range over which these species can be found. Their preferred optimum temperature will be somewhere between the two figures. The table is not alphabetical: species preferring cooler water are at the top, and those favoring warmer water at the bottom.

Temperature Preferences of Common Game Fish
Arctic grayling 42 to 50°F (5.55–10°C)
Arctic char 45 to 50°F (7.22–10°C)
Inconnu 48 to 50°F (8.88–10°C)
Mountain whitefish 46 to 52°F (7.77–11.11°C)
Lake trout 44 to 55°F (6.66–12.77°C)
Atlantic salmon 40 to 59°F (4.44–15°C)
Bull trout 45 to 55°F (7.22–12.77°C)
Cisco 45 to 55°F (7.22–12.77°C)
Coho salmon 44 to 60°F (6.66–15.55°C)
Lake whitefish 50 to 55°F (10–12.77°C)
Sockeye salmon 50 to 55°F (10–12.77°C)
Pink salmon 52 to 57°F (11.11–13.88°C)
Chum salmon 54 to 57°F (12.22–13.88°C)

Chinook salmon 50 to 63°F (10–17.22°C)

Brown trout 47 to 67°F (8.33–19.44°C)

Rainbow trout 47 to 67°F (8.33–19.44°C)

Paddlefish 55 to 60°F (12.77–15.55°C)

Cutthroat trout 55 to 62°F (12.77–16.66°C)

Golden trout 58 to 62°F (14.44–16.66°C)

Redeye bass 55 to 65°F (12.77–18.33°C)

Brook trout 47 to 67°F (8.33–19.44°C)

Northern pike 50 to 75°F (10–23.88°C)

Lake sturgeon 60 to 65°F (15.55–18.33°C)

Muskellunge 60 to 75°F (15.55–23.88°C)

Yellow perch 60 to 75°F (15.55–23.88°C)

Smallmouth bass 60 to 75°F (15.55–23.88°C)

Black crappie 60 to 75°F (15.55–23.88°C)

White crappie 60 to 75°F (15.55–23.88°C)

Chain pickerel 60 to 80°F (15.55–26.66°C)

Rock bass 69 to 74°F (20.55–23.33°C)

Largemouth bass 65 to 78°F (18.33–25.55°C)

Redear sunfish 65 to 80°F (18.33–26.66°C)

Bluegill 65 to 80°F (18.33–26.66°C)

Green sunfish 65 to 84°F (18.33–28.88°C)

Channel catfish 67 to 85°F (19.44–29.44°C)

Blue catfish 67 to 85°F (19.44–29.44°C)

Warmouth 80 to 85°F (26.66–29.44°C)

Most anglers don't carry thermometers in the field, but in a very general way, temperature can be estimated by dipping your hand in the water. If the water feels cool and not cold, the fish are likely to be more active and could be in the shallower stretches. If the water feels freezing cold, then try the deeper areas first.

In the heat of summer, it is more difficult to estimate temperature as the water always feels cold. Start fishing deep and work your way up toward the margins until the fish start biting.

Tight Lines
If the water feels cool and not cold, the fish are likely to be more active and could be in the shallower stretches. If the water feels freezing cold, then try the deeper areas first.

CHAPTER 3

Where the Fish Are When the Wind Blows and the Rain Falls

Wind and rain occur on any given day year-round, presenting the angler with new challenges and opportunities. It is important to understand how such events are likely to influence a day's fishing and be prepared to change tactics to optimize the chances of catching fish.

When the Breeze Blows

It would seem reasonable to assume that atmospheric pressure would be of little importance to fish, which are subject to comparatively huge changes in hydrostatic pressure within their aquatic environment. As we shall see, this is quite wrong because the barometer is responsible for weather events that influence fish in profound ways.

Atmospheric pressure is caused by the weight of the air around us pushing down on the earth's surface. The higher a lake or river is above sea level, the less air there is above it, and so the lower the air pressure.

As temperature drops, air cools and contracts, becoming denser and causing it to sink. Likewise, as it warms, it expands, becoming less dense and causing it to rise. Cooler air is thus virtually synonymous with higher air pressure, and warmer

Rain and wind have a profound influence on the aquatic environment and on fishes' behavior.

air with lower air pressure. As warm air rises away from the warmth of the earth's crust, it begins to cool and thus sink, while cool air next to the warm earth begins to warm and thus rise.

High barometric pressure is associated with settled weather, and low barometric pressure with wind and rain. Cool air is unable to hold as much water as warm air. As moist, warm air cools, the water begins to condense, forming clouds and eventually rain. As dry, cool air sinks and warms, it absorbs water and creates fine weather.

Wind is caused by the air attempting to balance out these differences in pressure. Air moves from areas of high pressure to areas of low pressure. Another way to view it is that if one light, warm mass of air rises, another heavier, cooler mass will inevitably move in sideways beneath it: there can't be *nothing* there. The greater the difference in atmospheric pressure between the adjacent high- and low-pressure centers, the stronger the winds will be.

Wind blowing over land works in a similar way to water flowing within a river. The wind close to the ground, like the water at the bottom of a river, passes the obstacles in its way and is slowed by friction. In a river, these obstacles are rocks and weeds; for the wind, they are trees, hills, and buildings. The wind or water passing high above these obstacles is free to travel much faster, as it is unobstructed. Wind passing over a flat body of water will often travel up to twice as fast as the same wind over a forest or city. Gusts occur as obstacles change the direction and speed of the wind.

Seasonal winds are caused by temperature differences on a global scale. As the earth revolves around the sun, the Northern and Southern hemispheres alternately receive more or less sunlight for months at a time, causing

Even a slight breeze creates surface water waves.

warming and cooling on a hemispheric basis. At the same time, the poles remain consistently cooler than the temperate zones, which in turn remain cooler than the tropics. Hot air over the tropics rises and travels north or south toward the poles before cooling, sinking, and returning to the equator. Due to the rotation of the earth, the wind usually moves generally in a west-to-east direction.

The alternation of day and night due to the earth's rotation also causes relatively rapid heating and cooling of different parts of the earth's surface, creating another, daily variable in the creation of winds.

There are also daily winds caused by differences in temperature between large bodies of water (seas and large lakes) and the land. Land heats up and cools down more quickly than water, causing air over land to warm faster than air over water. As warm air over land rises during the day, cooler air over water is sucked inland, creating a landward breeze. At night, air over the relatively warmer water warms and rises, causing the process to reverse. At sunset and sunrise, a period of calm occurs when the air temperatures are balanced above the land and the water and there is no movement unless caused by larger weather patterns beyond the immediate locale.

Before we turn to the effects of wind on fish, let's briefly mention one more pertinent effect of atmospheric pressure. As air pressure increases, local surface waters absorb more oxygen from the air, thus increasing the oxygen available to fish. As the barometer falls, the water releases oxygen into the air, becoming less oxygenated. As we saw in Chapter 2, changes in oxygen levels have significant implications for fish behavior and fishing.

Wind and Current

In a body of otherwise still water, friction between wind and the surface water causes drag, which eventually creates a surface current in the same direction as the wind. This in turn sets up a deeper current traveling in the opposite direction beneath the surface flow so that the surface remains essentially level at all times. Surface waters tend to flow at around 1 percent of the wind speed in the direction of the wind. The return undercurrent flows at a much slower speed, and its depth is greater than the comparatively shallow surface current.

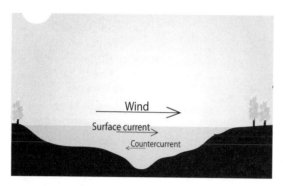

Wind generates a shallow surface current and a deeper, slower current below it flowing in the opposite direction.

These currents influence the behavior of fish. After a period of wind blowing from one direction, the fish can almost always be found feeding on the lee shore. This is because the food on the surface is driven by the currents toward the lee bank, where it gathers and is readily consumed by awaiting fish. Although fishing these banks is more difficult (as the angler has to cast into the wind), it is always worth the trouble.

As a side point, those movements along the surface waters on squally days that appear to be fish darting swiftly beneath the surface are in fact often simply gusts of wind shifting the surface waters and not, as it is easy to be fooled into believing, fish sliding past just under the surface.

In addition to wind-generated currents, the winds themselves blowing toward the bank can push the water up against the land. These conditions can

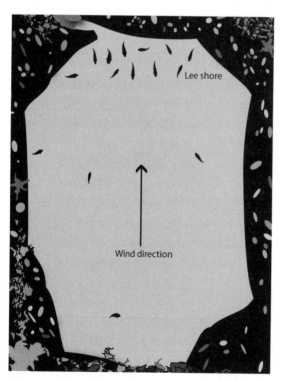

Fish will normally be found feeding on the lee shore when the wind picks up.

force less mobile organisms such as fish fry, terrestrial insects, and plankton closer to shore. These prey items bring large numbers of fish of all sizes into the shallows and inevitably attract the bigger fish. As a general rule, the stronger the winds, the shallower these fish will be forced to venture.

Wind Lanes

Surface currents on lakes and ponds often organize themselves into distinctly visible "wind lanes," which collect and trap debris and food items at the water's surface. Fish are very much aware of this potential food source and can often be seen rising around the lanes to pick off a fly or food particle they have observed from below the surface. These can be very productive places to fish, although they generally need to be accessed by boat. The best methods around wind lanes are flies dropped either on or just below the surface. Imitating the naturals found in the air at the time you fish should bring good results.

Erosion

Wind also shapes the environment in which fish live on a more permanent basis. A lake shoreline regularly battered by wind-driven waves will be eroded and lack bankside vegetation. A sheltered shoreline, on the other hand, will have much richer plant life growing along it. Consequently, the windward, not the leeward, shore may offer more productive fishing during those times of day when fish seek shelter and are not aggressively on the feed.

> **Tight Lines**
> The windward shore may offer more productive fishing during those times of day when fish seek shelter.

Waves, Temperature, and Oxygen

Wind is a strong factor in determining the temperature of the water in shallow areas, such as open coastal reaches and exposed lake margins—more so than in deeper waters. Strong winds increase the mixing between the water and the air and tend to cool shallow surface waters. As we have seen, temperature changes have a strong influence on the behavior of fish, and this is yet another mechanism by which winds can influence where fish are likely to be found.

Wind-driven waves break when they reach shallow water, which generally appears close to shorelines. The shallowing bottom acts like a brake, slowing the forward motion of the deeper water by friction while the wave crest continues at full speed. As the top of the wave rushes forward and the bottom slows down, the wave "trips" over itself and breaks. The stronger the winds, the larger the waves. This increases the water's oxygen level, due to the mechanical mixing effect. The increase in oxygen is in addition to the increase in the water's oxygen-holding capacity caused by the cooling effect of the wind. A third, more occasional cooling effect can occur if the wind blows snow from the surrounding banks into the water.

Wind and Fish Activity

There is some evidence that certain species of fish are more active at higher wind speeds. The critical wind speed above which fish activity was found to increase is 8 meters per second (18 miles per hour). This is the speed at which the wind begins to cause significant changes to the subsurface water.

Another possible explanation for fishes' increased activity during high winds could be that the wind knocks airborne insects from the sky into the surface water. Using a net towed from a biplane, scientists have estimated that each cubic mile of sky may contain as many as twenty-five million insects, spiders, and other invertebrates; even relatively large animals like grasshoppers can be carried by wind over huge distances. Many of these invertebrates are unable to escape the surface film once they hit the water. As described earlier, if not eaten outright, they are then pushed by the wind toward the lee shore, where they collect into a smorgasbord for the fish.

In the North Atlantic Ocean, between 40°N and 60°N, the swell heads eastward almost constantly, driven by

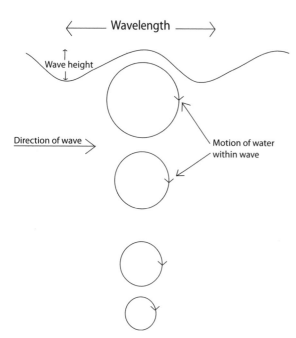

Waves create vertical circulation far below the surface.

the prevailing winds. Early seafarers used this information as a reliable navigational aid for centuries. There is some evidence that fish too are able to use the direction of swells to find their way around, even at a fair depth. Within a small lake or river, this would not be possible (or necessary), but in much larger bodies of water, it would be very useful. Fish certainly have the ability to sense the direction the wind is blowing at the surface, and as shown in the figure on page 72, the movement at the surface affects the water for some distance below it.

When the Rain Falls

Rain can give some of the best catches of all weather phenomena. It seems to have the ability to turn fish into feeding machines. For the angler who knows how to make the most out of the rain, such times can provide the best sport available. Be aware, though, that it is during these severe weather conditions that the angler is at most risk, and several anglers are killed by lightning every year while fishing in rain.

> **Tight Lines**
> Rain seems to have the ability to turn fish into feeding machines.

During heavy rainfall, it is not uncommon to have multiple takes in quick succession. Clearly, fish feed at the surface during rainstorms, but why do they feed so aggressively? There are many reasons for this, including the following:

▶ Rain increases the water's oxygen levels, boosting the fishes' energy.

▶ Rain causes dramatic physical changes to the underwater environment, resulting in an overload of sensory inputs that may excite or confuse fish.

▶ Rain introduces a rare bounty and variety of food items into the fishes' reach.

▶ Given that the increased food source occurs simultaneously with the increased risk of predation, fish strive to eat as much as possible as quickly as possible.

▶ When a number of fish try to eat large amounts in a short period of time, it leads to competition for food between individuals, especially within schools, giving further impetus to rapid feeding.

Fish have the ability to learn that rain can bring food. Anyone who has kept a goldfish will have seen how excited fish can become when exposed to any stimulus that can be regularly associated with food. This is summed up in one experiment in which a zoologist who fed his minnows in a special aquarium compartment would regularly blow a whistle before feeding them. Before long, they would become noticeably excited as soon as they heard the whistle, racing into their feeding chamber even when he did not feed them.

He also blew a second whistle with a different tone, after which he touched the fish with a stick. (He did this carefully so as not to injure them, but they clearly found it unpleasant and avoided it when possible.) They soon learned to hide in reaction to the "stick" tone and race to their feeding chamber after hearing the feeding tone. These experiments clearly demonstrated the fishes' ability to react appropriately when faced with different environmental stimuli.

Predators and Food

It is no accident that horror films exploit thunderstorms the way they do. The senses of all animals are temporarily impaired under these noisy, light-scattering conditions, making them more vulnerable to lurking predators. Observations have shown that lions hunt more and make more kills during storms, and it is reasonable to assume that all predators take advantage of any situation that makes catching prey easier. During heavy downpours, predatory fish come out from the cover of weed beds and lurk below the surface, ready to strike at prey.

Fish do not normally feed in places where the risk of predation is high, but when they are hungry, fish take more risks and spend more time foraging in comparatively dangerous places. This suggests that fish are aware of the food sources in these areas but are inhibited from reaching them by their instinctive fear of predation. If heavy rainfall reduces fishes' ability to detect predators, why would they feed during a rainstorm?

One reason is the greater quantity of food available. On calm days, the surface film acts like a spider's web, conveniently trapping insects for fish to feed on. The number of insects flying above a large area of fresh water at any given time is considerable, and heavy rain knocks even more of these insects out of the air and into the water. While the rain's sensory distractions increase the risk side of the fish's calculation, the enhanced availability of food raises the rewards as well.

The number of insects in the water at any given time is dependent on many weather variables. During summer, the number of insects available to be knocked down is much greater than in winter. A large number of insects mate in flight during the summer, presenting targets that are approximately twice as large (and providing a double meal for a lucky fish). As mentioned earlier, low-pressure air that accompanies storms is less dense than high-pressure air and is therefore more difficult to fly in, increasing the number of weaker insects falling onto the water. Of course, wind strength and the volume and heaviness of rainfall are important variables. It is a little-known fact that raindrops are not the familiar teardrop shape, but actually the shape of a wobbling coin. This shape covers a greater area than the teardrop shape would and is more likely to hit anything passing beneath it. Rain clears the air by physically knocking its contents to the ground. This is one of the reasons going for a run during a thunderstorm feels so good.

Even as the risks from predatory fish are increased, the overall risk of predation during a storm may be reduced in some fisheries or for some species. As direct sunlight is blocked off by clouds, the water appears more opaque from above, impairing the ability of fish-eating birds to locate feeding fish. On calm days, fish are able to see the whole horizon above the water reflected at an angle of about 98 degrees. This means that a predator approaching from above cannot be seen until it is directly above the fish. When wind drives the surface into waves, this window is broken up, and fish get a scattered view of birds approaching from a greater distance. Anglers should keep this phenomenon (known as "Snell's window") in mind, for it also makes them more visible than usual from the bank. The proper response is to move as far as possible from the water's edge or to hide behind a feature like a large rock or tree trunk.

Many anglers claim that trout rise during stormy conditions because they believe the raindrops are food pellets being thrown onto the water surface. For wild trout, this explanation would not make sense, but many modern fisheries are stocked with hatchery-raised trout. In order for a learned response to perpetuate, it needs to be continuously reinforced; that is, food must be presented frequently, immediately after raindrops hit the surface. If this is not the case—as after hatchery-bred fish are released into the wild and are no longer fed pellets—this behavior will die out. In other words, if fish had not already learned that rain and pellets were unrelated while in the fish farm, they would learn this almost as soon as they were released into the wild. The fact that rain itself brings food to the fish complicates matters but does not change the lack of association between pellets and rain; the fish are associating the rain with food and not necessarily pellets.

> **Tight Lines**
> When wind drives the surface into waves, fish not only get a scattered view of birds approaching from a greater distance, but also of anglers on the bank.

High Oxygen Levels and Sensory Overload

Rain increases oxygen levels in the water, due to mechanical mixing, and often because rain is colder than the bodies of water into which it falls. By reducing the water's temperature, rain increases its capacity to hold dissolved oxygen. Higher oxygen levels naturally result in an increase in fishes' activity.

Near the surface, heavy rain causes a major change in the aquatic environment, subjecting fish there to sensory overload. When viewed from below the surface, the water seems to "erupt" from above, as shown in the photograph on page 77, reducing visibility in the first few inches of depth. Acoustically, the pounding raindrops and escaping bubbles drown out other sounds. The turbulent battering of the rain severely reduces the efficiency of the fish's lateral line. Even fishes' sense of smell can be influenced by the odor of fresh solutes filling the water around them. It is likely that such a combination of sensory inputs excites fish, possibly causing them to snap at potential food items without spending time observing them. This is a time to use brightly colored flies and baits just below the surface to draw the fish's attention under these visually constrained conditions.

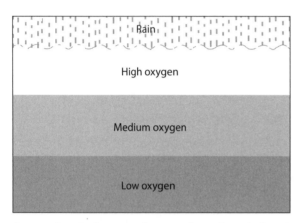

Oxygen levels rise near the water's surface during rainfall.

Tight Lines
During heavy rains, use brightly colored flies and baits just below the surface to draw the attention of fish excited by the sensory input overload and therefore more likely to snap at food offerings without inspecting.

The winds associated with rain stir the surface of the water, causing it to become less transparent. Under choppy conditions, the convex parts of the water surface (when viewed from above) focus the light downward, creating bright spots, while concave areas disperse the light, creating dark blotches. Overall, however, dark skies associated with rain reduce the intensity of light under water. Lacking eyelids, the eyes of trout are easily damaged by bright sunlight, so dark weather enables them to forage more comfortably at or near the surface.

As mentioned earlier, one biologist found that minnows became excited as light levels fell below a certain level. They were observed breaking the surface and even jumping clear of the water. This excitement seemed to have little to do with feeding. Perhaps fish just enjoy the changing conditions?

Action at the Margins

As well as scattering insects over the surface of the water, rain stirs up the silt in the shallow margins, releasing invertebrates hiding within it.

This turbulence has the added bonus of making the water cloudy. Fish have been found to seek out turbid

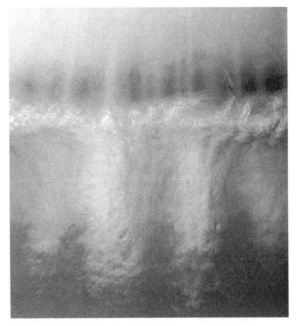

A fish's-eye view of heavy rain.

water when placed in clear water. This is thought to be a mechanism for predator avoidance. The combined allure of bottom-dwelling invertebrates and protection from predators is likely to draw fish toward the banks.

Rain also brings terrestrial worms to the surface to escape flooding burrows; these and other land invertebrates are often washed into the water by runoff from the surrounding land, adding to the food sources available at the margins. It is always worth placing an imitation terrestrial, worm, or slug right in the margins during periods of heavy rainfall. Try to aim for the colored water where the runoff is entering the lake.

In shallow water, rain stirs up the sediment and exposes food.

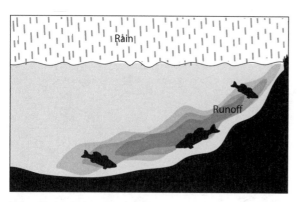

Runoff can bring food and cover to the margins and attract fish.

Rising water levels associated with prolonged bouts of rain will expose new feeding grounds to the resident fish. When this happens, the fish move right into the new, expanded margins. A common mistake anglers make is to wade out and cast into the open water. If the water level has just risen, the cast should be made parallel to the banks. Although aquatic imitations do work at this time, terrestrial flies or baits are likely to work better.

Fish can be driven off the feed by heavy rain in certain circumstances. Marine fish, for example, tend to stop feeding during heavy rainfall. There are fewer insects above the sea than over lakes and rivers, so one of the main inducements to feed in the rain is absent, while the risk of predation is heightened.

> **Tight Lines**
> A common mistake anglers make is to wade out and cast into the open water. If the water level has just risen, the cast should be made parallel to the banks.

The Problem of pH

The pH value of water indicates its acid or base (i.e., alkaline) content. Above pH 7.6, water is alkaline, and below pH 6.8, it is acidic. Most natural lakes have a pH of between 6 and 9.

The "hardness" of water is a measure of its mineral content. The most common minerals found in water—calcium and magnesium—are both alkaline. Hard waters usually contain relatively high levels of calcium and are therefore less prone to acidification. Soft waters contain little calcium and are susceptible to acidification.

In fresh water, heavy rainfall can briefly but dramatically increase the acidity of the water. It may also increase the concentration of toxic trace metals such as aluminum, lead, zinc, and manganese. The rise and ensuing fall of these environmental factors can occur over very short periods, even minutes, and obviously depends upon the geology and chemistry of the surrounding area and upon the water's current pH.

Although rain is normally slightly acidic, acid rain is produced when burning fossil fuels release sulphur- and nitrogen-containing gases into the atmosphere. As rain falls, it cleans the air of these pollutants by picking up suspended particles. The rain, thus acidified, then falls into bodies of water either directly or via runoff.

Sadly, only about 10 percent of the constituents of acid rain come from natural sources such as forest fires and volcanoes; the other 90 percent are caused by man. The problem is made worse by the fact that pollutants are often carried thousands of miles from their point of origin before being deposited into beautiful and otherwise unpolluted lakes and rivers. Fish secrete mucus around their gills to protect themselves from the water's acidity, but in extreme cases, so much mucus may be produced as to impair the gills' function, effectively smothering the fish and leading to large-scale kills (especially in salmonids) within hours of the onset of rain.

It is well documented that the growth of trout is generally good in alkaline waters and poor in acidic waters, but this is due to the comparatively rapid growth of invertebrates under alkaline conditions, producing more food for the trout. What influence could a short-term change in pH have on the behavior of trout?

Trout avoid acidic waters by seeking deeper water or, in river systems, moving away from the unfavorable areas. Rain that is significantly more acidic than the water into which it falls can cause the fish to stop feeding. Since you may not be equipped to test the water's pH on the spot when traveling, ask local anglers about the influence of rain on a particular fishery.

Low pH has been shown to reduce or eliminate feeding by interfering with chemoreception (essential to the senses of smell and taste) and therefore the fish's ability to locate food. It is best

> **Tight Lines**
> Ask local anglers about the influence of rain on a particular fishery, especially in regard to pH levels. It is best to avoid acidified waters when fishing, as the fish are unlikely to be located here, and those that remain will not be feeding as actively as fish in other areas.

Acidified waters interfere with fishes' ability to find food.

to avoid acidified waters when fishing, as the fish are unlikely to be located here, and those that remain will not be feeding as actively as fish in other areas.

Trout and salmon are extremely sensitive to low pH levels, while perch and pike are among the most acid-tolerant species and are often the last two species present in an acidified lake. Your selection of, or readiness to change, fishing location based on acidity should therefore be influenced by the species you are targeting.

Rain can have serious consequences for intertidal (the area of shoreline between low and high tide) fish sitting out low tide in a rock pool. The rain falling onto the rocks reduces salinity within the pools. As a result, rock-pool-dwelling fish have evolved a tolerance, much higher than that of other fish species, to changes in salinity and temperature and are able to survive in this harsh environment.

The physical aftermath of severe storms often has devastating effects on coastal fish. Fish that survive the crushing forces of the waves and rocks have further problems. The crashing waves stir up sand and other larger debris into suspension, and the suspended sediment tears at fishes' gills and eyes, leaving many smaller fish blinded by the scratching or suffocated by their torn gill filaments. Larger fish are less affected by the abrasive materials, as their gills are larger and the membranes covering their eyes thicker, and they are often attracted to the coast following such a storm in large numbers to feed on the corpses of the dead. For this reason dead-baiting can be very effective after a powerful storm.

Freshwater predators like pike move into the cloudy inlet areas of a lake in search of food washed in by the downpour. As this environment is turbid, their vision will be impaired. It is always a good idea to use bait with a strong scent or a lure with an intense vibration. The fish are much more likely to find your hook if you present the baits in this way.

> **Tight Lines**
> It is always a good idea to use bait with a strong scent or a lure with an intense vibration after a heavy storm.

Always seek out the areas where the water is most colored. This is where the feeding fish are likely to congregate.

Fishing in Rain

When not fishing the margins during heavy rainfall, the angler should present his or her bait in open surface water: that's where the predators are waiting. Use a

(a) These buoyant surface lures have flattened faces that create turbulence and prevent them from diving during a retrieve. (b) In contrast, the diving vane on the front of this lure will pull the lure down into the water: the faster the retrieve, the deeper it will dive.

slow retrieve and keep the plug just below the surface, giving the fish ample time to spot it.

When fly-fishing in heavy rain, put a buoyant fly on the point and a smaller colorful terrestrial pattern on the dropper.

After the onset of rain, any surviving insects seek shelter, only returning to the air once the weather has cleared. Patchy weather with repeating, heavy showers followed by mild sunny spells cause more insects to be caught out than one long downpour. For this reason, flying-insect imitations may be worthwhile in patchy weather.

When float-fishing, use fatter floats. The extra buoyancy can be helpful. It will keep the float clear of the water, making it more visible. Painting the upper side of a float bright red or orange will make it much easier to see through the downpour than conventional stick floats.

Use a buoyant point fly and a sinking dropper to keep your flies in the surface waters.

A bobber or float made from a wine-bottle cork is ideal for heavy rain.

Turbid Water

Water is turbid when it has picked up and is carrying a sediment load. This can be caused when the flow rate is increased or storm or flood events cause severe mixing and stirring up of sediments into the water column.

Fish will sometimes hide themselves in turbid water.

Because turbid water carries a sediment load, the physical properties of the water are changed. Light penetration is restricted by the presence of the sediment particles, and for this reason, turbid water often provides a hiding place for fish. Once the flow rate slows and mixing is reduced, the water will once again drop the sediment load to the river or lake bed, and as a result, the clarity of the water will increase.

One interesting experiment showed how turbid water changes the behavior of salmon, where it was noted that although most evidence points to turbidity reducing the fish's visual ability, fish often seek out turbid conditions. Some of the greatest Pacific salmon-producing rivers are highly turbid. It was concluded that the turbidity protected the young salmon from their visual predators, as the majority of piscivorous (i.e., fish-eating) birds and fish use vision when hunting.

The researcher used life-size rubber models of fish predators (dogfish and gull) and measured the avoidance response of juvenile chinook salmon. It was found that the young salmon were startled by the presence of predators. They darted into the deeper regions of the tank. Interestingly, more salmon hid in response to the presence of the gull than the dogfish. The salmon also took

A well-camouflaged fish-eating bird observes the water from the top of a tree.

much longer to recover after the sighting of the gull (an average of 3.8 minutes) than of the dogfish (an average of 0.4 minutes). In clear water, almost all of the fish swam into the deeper region of the tank when faced with either predator. In turbid water, the number of fish darting for cover was reduced. It was also noticed that the recovery period was six times longer in clear water than in turbid water.

So in very cloudy water, fish feel safer from predators, as they are less likely to be seen. Turbid water reduces the long-distance visibility of fish. It can, however (on bright days), improve a fish's ability to spot prey when swimming a few centimeters away from it. This environment is ideal for foraging fish because they are able to see their prey while remaining out of the view of any predators lurking in the distance. Under these conditions, foraging fish selectively search for the slower species and ignore the faster ones. Faster prey items are more difficult to catch as they are able to dart out of the fish's reach back into the gloom of the cloudy water before being snapped up.

In turbid water, the light is scattered by the particles within the water. This environment changes the way objects appear. In very bright conditions, the scattered sunlight can illuminate prey from all directions, enhancing its visibility at this close range. As soon as the fish swims past the prey, it quickly becomes obscured again by the cloudy water.

As we shall see, turbid water may make fish feel safer, but it can also play into the hands of their predators.

Turbid Water and Predatory Ambush

Prey fish like young salmon and trout actively seek out cloudy water. Predatory fish like northern pike, largemouth bass, and muskellunge mainly hunt by sight and so would normally be hunting in clear water. Knowing, as anglers do, that cloudy waters mean fish, predatory fish have learned to sit and wait in ambush in these areas. Although they cannot see the fish, the pike use their lateral line to feel the water around them. If an unsuspecting fish gets too close, then they strike. For anglers, the lesson here is to use a large plug and fish it slowly, covering plenty of water. Preference should be given to those plugs with internal vibration or wobbling wakes.

> **Tight Lines**
> Use a large plug with internal vibrations or wobbling wakes, and fish it slowly when covering turbid waters.

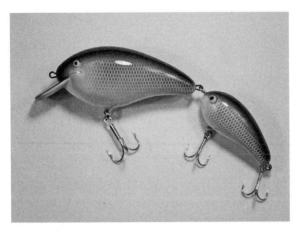

This jointed lure not only creates attractive turbulence as it wiggles through the water, but it also contains metal ball bearings that rattle as it moves.

To summarize, then, there are two reasons why fish feed regularly in areas of cloudy water. The first, referred to as the *physical effect hypothesis*, is the tendency of turbidity to increase the contrast between the prey and its surroundings, increasing the fish's ability to spot the prey. The second is the *motivation hypothesis*, whereby the increasing turbidity levels lead to a decrease in the perceived risk of the fish being eaten by predators and therefore increase its motivation to feed.

Scent is not impaired by turbid water providing it is not contaminated in any way. Obviously, during the night, the turbid areas do not influence the position of the fish, as in the darkness, they do not feel so vulnerable. The source of the turbidity may still draw in fish at night if it increases the food available to them, but as the fish are in darkness anyway, they will not alter their feeding behavior as they enter the turbid water.

A northern pike lurks in ambush.

Fish close to the surface with scented baits in turbid water and start moving down until the fish bite. This way it is possible to cover the water most likely to hold fish first and also provide the angler with a mechanism for measuring the depth (by counting as the bait sinks before the retrieve). Once a fish is hooked, it is then possible to cast a second time to the same depth (by counting to the same number). One way to attract fish in these conditions is to avoid the problems associated with vision and pull the fish in using a different sense. This is why strong-smelling bait can be very effective.

> **Tight Lines**
> Fish close to the surface with scented baits in turbid water, and start moving down until the fish bite.

When fly-fishing cloudy water, try to imitate slower prey species and try to twitch the flies along slowly, allowing the fish to grab them before they pass through into the darkness. Flies with gold heads or metallic threads will pick up and reflect what little light is available, increasing the chances of them being spotted by the passing fish.

Sharks and Storms

Sharks normally need to keep swimming in order to pass adequate oxygen over their gills. The waters near ocean shorelines are often highly oxygenated due to wave action, and these areas provide a haven for sharks in which they can rest motionless while still obtaining adequate oxygen. Freshwater fish, too, make the most of these oxygen-rich, cooler periods.

Research has even shown that rain can increase shark attacks on people. As mentioned earlier, rainfall washes dirt and dust particles into water systems and is often associated with choppy weather that stirs up sediment that had previously settled on the bottom. The mouths of rivers and streams are particularly dangerous places as the residue from inland is washed out to sea. Sharks are attracted to such areas, as carcasses are often washed into the water. Under these low-visibility conditions, sharks often mistake people for their prey and attack.

The rogue shark theory has come about as a result of the repeated occurrence of clusters of attacks in the same area over a short time. For this reason, they are often referred to as the "attacks of 1916," or whenever that particular cluster of attacks occurred. Scientists studying sharks have found that they do not remain in the same place for long, traveling huge distances over relatively short periods of time. This has led to speculation about the causes of such attack events. It is more likely that these attacks are the result of rogue weather conditions and not rogue sharks. Sharks have been shown to confuse people for their normal prey under specific weather conditions. During prolonged periods of such conditions, it becomes more and more likely that any shark passing through a certain area would mistakenly attack a swimmer. The individual shark doing the attacking is different each time, but the environmental conditions encouraging the attacks remain similar.

Severe Weather and Lightning

It is often the case that what occurs in fresh water also occurs in the ocean but on a larger scale. Similar to insects being brought down over fresh water during rainstorms is the common incidence of migrating birds, tired from their grueling journey, being brought down into the sea in huge numbers by ocean storms. This is particularly devastating when hailstones are involved. On a much smaller scale, lightning can dance between birds in a flock and kill dozens of them at a time, dropping their bodies into the surface waters below. Similar to insects knocked into fresh water, this abundance of drowned or exhausted birds would be a source of food for fish in the open ocean.

Waterspouts occur regularly on oceans, large lakes, and rivers. These phenomena are spiraling updrafts of air that suck water into the clouds. They are powerful enough to lift the largest of freshwater fish, and whole schools of surface-dwelling species can be sucked up and pulled high into the air. The waterspout may carry them miles inland before depositing them with the rain. A large variety of animals have been recorded falling with the rain, many of which are gregarious and so fall in huge numbers. Rains of fish, tadpoles, frogs, toads, snails, crayfish, plants, maggots, bivalves, birds, snakes, and even turtles have all been recorded. Due to the forces involved, most animals transported in this way are dead on arrival. A few individuals are, however, likely to survive. Fascinatingly, before knowledge of tectonic plates and the movements of the earth's crust, these fish falls were used to explain the presence of fossilized fish on mountaintops.

A theory currently being hotly debated is the idea that thunderstorms tend to follow rivers and other waterways. There is a great deal of controversy, with some scientists believing this to be true because of the way the air is channeled in these regions, but others are doubtful. If this is the case, then fish are more likely to be exposed to rain than terrestrial animals.

As you read this, there are two thousand thunderstorms occurring around the globe, and lightning is striking the earth somewhere one hundred times a second. We know that lightning can kill anglers, but it can also harm fish in several ways. The sudden changes in air pressure caused as the lightning strikes reduce the oxygen levels within the surface waters and can lead to fish kills. A strike can heat the surrounding air to 54,032°F (30,000°C). Thunder is the result of the super-heated air expanding violently. When a bolt strikes water, any nearby fish are electrocuted, and the resulting shock wave can cause fish mortalities farther away. The diameter of fish kills around the impact site depends on the force of the strike, but the energy is quickly absorbed and so the kills tend to be fairly restricted.

Predicting Storms in the Field

One way to discover the imminent arrival of an approaching storm is by observing changes in other animals. Sea birds are instinctively aware of the imminence of a serious storm, sheltering on land or remaining close to shore long before it arrives. It is certain that they are using some aspect of their immediate environment in order to detect its presence. If birds are able to use this early warning system, then it is possible that fish have evolved the ability to recognize the signs of an approaching storm too.

> **Tight Lines**
> Increasing humidity and the appearance of vapor trails behind jet planes are both precursors of rain.

Increasing humidity is another precursor of rain, so an additional weather clue, for humans, is the appearance of vapor trails behind jet planes. Aircraft may disturb the peace while you're sitting by a beautiful river or lake, but their passing overhead can have its uses. When a plane leaves a lasting vapor trail, or contrail, the air contains more moisture, and this could suggest the onset of rain. When the trail disappears quickly, the air is dry, and the weather is likely to remain stable.

During the night, use the stars as a guide. They twinkle more when the air is humid.

The persistence of a jet's vapor trail is an indicator of the amount of moisture in the atmosphere.

CHAPTER **4**

Where the Fish Are Through the Seasons

The passing of the seasons causes dramatic changes in the suitability of particular habitats for fish. Short-term weather changes throughout the year, but it is important for the angler to view the influence of the daily weather in the context of seasonal change. Certain short-term changes can have different implications for fish behavior at different times of year.

Seasonality means different things in different parts of the world. In the extreme north, for example, the sun completely disappears from October to February, while near the equator, light levels barely change with the seasons. Winter may be dry and cold in some regions, but in others, it may be pleasantly cool but consistently rainy. Although the nature and severity of seasonal weather differ from one place to another, overall, seasonal changes inevitably have a large impact on the aquatic environment. As discussed below, these changes include the following:

- ▶ Long-term changes in water temperature
- ▶ Long-term changes in the water's oxygen content
- ▶ Changes in food availability and location
- ▶ Changes in water level, speed of current, and turbidity
- ▶ Presence or absence of ice

These changing conditions expose fish to discomfort and danger at certain times of the year, forcing them to move out of an area in which they had previously been comfortable. At other times, changing conditions offer rewards, such as new food sources or cover, that provide positive inducements to enter a new area. Generally, during the spring, fish move out of the deeper water where they have been over-wintering and seek fresh feeding grounds. In the heat of summer, they are forced back into the deeper water or beneath overhanging cover to escape from the sun's heat. Autumn brings them into the shallows again before they descend into the depths for the winter.

In keeping with these very general seasonal patterns of behavior, one can make equally broad generalizations about fishing strategies to suit. In cold weather, when fish are less active, use bigger baits and static or slow-moving baits, and fish close to where the fish will be. Move around and bring your bait to them, because they will be moving less. During the summer, faster retrieves and brighter colors can encourage energetic fish to lunge for the hook.

Knowing where your chosen fish will be at any time of year is half the battle. A little research can save hours wasted at the bank flogging dead water.

> **Tight Lines**
> Use bigger, slow-moving baits in cold weather and bright-colored fast retrieves in the heat.

Seasonal Preferences

Fish generally feed much more in the spring and summer than in the fall and winter. This is due not so much to changes in the quantity of food that is available, but to shifts in their metabolism made in reaction to changes in water temperature. As described in Chapter 1, cold temperature causes fishes' metabolic rates to drop, reducing both their overall level of activity and the energy they need.

Fish species that live in fast-flowing water try to conserve energy in cold weather. On a short-term basis, trout that habitually hide behind boulders will pull in even lower and closer behind their refuge to reduce the energy needed to hold position. They are unlikely at these times to move far from the cover of their refuges. They will, however, feed if a tempting meal appears sufficiently close to their home rock to collect without a large expenditure of energy.

When the weather turns cold for long periods, as during the winter, stream-dwelling fish move away from their summer feeding grounds and seek the deeper, warmer water of a nearby pool. Several fish will live in the same pool, and those pools that are covered by overhanging trees or bridges tend to be the most popular, as these features provide fish with cover from predators. In these refuges, fish are less likely to move around, so you will have to. Use lightweight tackle so you can be mobile and cover more water. Cast upstream of the pool and allow the bait to topple over the rocks in the shallow water before falling into the pool. This will appear more natural to the resident fish.

Fish living in lakes also seek deeper water in winter. It is useful to look at maps or seek local advice, as the deepest water in a lake is rarely in the middle. There are often deeper pockets scattered over the lake bed, and these will provide the most productive fishing.

Many riverine species of fish, including brown trout and common carp, prefer to remain in one place during the winter months, only moving when forced to do so. In extreme cases, ice dams can begin to fill the deep pools. In such cases, the fish may be forced to leave the pools and seek refuge from the current along the margins of the river where the flow is at its slowest. It is always worth giving these marginal swims a cast to see if they hold any sheltering fish. This is particularly the case if the margins are deeper than usual. In most cases when the ice dams melt, the fish return to their original pools.

Fish seek deeper water during extremes of temperature.

A surge in fish activity occurs as the seasons change and the water begins to warm up, and spring can provide excellent fishing. But there are limits. During the hottest months (July and August in the Northern Hemisphere), fish seek refuge from the heat and the sun's glare by retreating again to the cooler, deeper pools.

When overwintering riverine species like trout return to their summer feeding grounds, the biggest fish compete for the best territories. In warmer waters, the

Tight Lines
Use smaller flies during the summer. Move around to other areas if you don't have quick success.

fish now have more energy and are more likely to move away from their "home" rock to hunt or forage. As we discussed before, it is worth remembering that a trout's home range averages about a 40-meter stretch of river, and trout living in small streams will often travel around 10 meters away from their home range to feed. At this time of year, smaller flies can be used. Start fishing as soon as you arrive at the riverbank, and if you don't have quick success, move to another area promptly. As the fish will be on the move, most spots have a chance of yielding a strike.

Just as humans rely on seasonal crops, fish too have an annual cycle of food items, and they feed on what is most abundant at the time. As other aquatic species live out their life cycles, they become more or less exposed to feeding fish. The classic example of this are the periods of fly hatches along a river at the onset of spring and the abundance of many species of fish fry in the margins. For example, brown trout spawn in the winter, and the fry of any fish provides another source of food for many species of fish. Fish will feed on fry when they are around. Equally,

A vast array of fly patterns has been developed to appeal to fishes' habitual diet at every period of the year.

conditions can remove a source of food from the fishes' reach. When surface ice completely covers a lake, terrestrial organisms become unobtainable.

It is easy to find life-cycle tables listing which invertebrates are present at different times of the year, and numerous "match the hatch" books are available in most bookstores and tackle shops, but due to differences between individual rivers and lakes, these are very general guides at best. It is more useful to take a dip net to your local fishery and see what is around. There is every chance that if you can catch it with a net, so can the trout. But it is possible to get an even more accurate view, not just of what's available, but of what the fish are actually feeding on. If you are fishing for the pot, you can examine the stomach contents of your fish after you gut it. If not, you can use a marrow spoon or a turkey baster to carefully take a sample from the trout's stomach and observe the contents. Place the contents into water to separate them,

> **Tight Lines**
> Examine the stomach contents of your catch after you gut it. If one food item is prevalent, use an imitation of it when fishing for that species.

and you will be able to see the different species that the fish has eaten and, perhaps more importantly, their relative abundance. If there is a preponderance of one species in the fish's stomach, use an imitation of this when fishing for the same species.

Studies carried out on the stomach contents of lake- and river-dwelling trout reveal a varied diet throughout the year. In a study conducted in the Northern Hemisphere, lake trout consumed large numbers of freshwater shrimp (*Gammarus*) in January, February, and March. During the same period, river-

The young of amphibians also provide a seasonal feast for fish.

ine trout consumed mainly stone fly nymphs. During April, May, and June, the lake trout consumed mainly freshwater shrimp and caddis fly larvae, while the river dwellers concentrated on stone fly nymphs, midge larvae, and mayfly nymphs. In July, August, and September, the lake trout consumed large quantities of caddis fly and midge larvae, as well as a significant number of terrestrial insects (including grasshoppers, ants, beetles, and caterpillars), while the river-dwelling trout fed

A caterpillar washed into the water provides fish with a tasty meal.

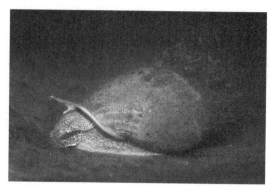

Young freshwater snails are eaten by many species of fish.

predominantly on terrestrial insects and midge larvae. (The river trout consumed more terrestrial insects than the lake trout.) In October, November, and December, the lake trout consumed almost no terrestrial insects but huge numbers of water slaters (*Asellus*) and shrimp. Throughout the same three months, the river trout consumed a small number of terrestrials, but their main diet consisted of stone fly nymphs. The lake trout also consumed large numbers of aquatic snails (*Lymnaea*) in February and October. The point here is that two populations of the same species of fish can feed on different things depending on what is about where they live.

Floods

Like most things in fishing, and in life, there are two sides to flooding. Flooding exposes fish to the dangers of strong currents and moving debris, forcing them out of their preferred habitats and making them spend extra energy to do so. But it also introduces them to new territories with new food sources. Although flooding can damage the eggs and young of fish that have already spawned, it is a vital cleaning process for the spawning beds of trout and other fish. Perch, for example, prefer to spawn on dead branches and roots washed into the water by rising water levels.

During flooding, water breaks the riverbanks and spreads over the surrounding land. Floods can erase the boundaries between rivers and neighboring lakes, allowing different species of fish to enter new waters and increase their genetic diversity. It is for this reason that extreme care should be taken when stocking

A northern pike explores new ground during a flood.

lakes and ponds situated on a floodplain. Any flooding could allow them to spread into and mix with wild populations, potentially causing serious damage through disease, competition, and interbreeding.

The timing of flooding can determine which fish species are dominant the following year. For example, the population size of brown and rainbow trout within a stream are determined in part by the arrival of that year's flooding. Spring floods cause a reduction in the numbers of the spring-spawning rainbow trout, while winter floods cause a reduction in the number of the winter-spawning brown trout. As a result of the lower numbers of one species, the surviving trout of the other species do better than normal because they do not have to compete as aggressively for food and territory.

Slight Flooding

The severity of flooding also makes a significant difference in fishes' habitat and behavior. More water means more living space for fish. It also means new feeding grounds.

Current

During flooding, fish seek out the shelter of backwaters.

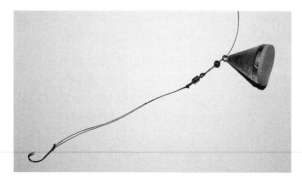

This leger rig allows the bait to float, while the flat base of the weight keeps it in position, preventing it from rolling around and snagging in the weeds.

When water levels within a stream rise, the fish within the pools come out and feed in the shallower stretches previously inaccessible to them. When the water velocity increases, the fish will retreat into areas of slower flow. Many fish species will move downstream, returning to their home grounds when the water level returns to normal. More water generally makes fish more confident. They will travel slightly farther and be more ready to move for a meal. For the angler, however, more water and higher flows cover up underwater features, making it more difficult to locate the fish.

As waters rise farther and currents increase, new riparian stretches become available. Fish will readily move out of the riverbed and into these areas, not so much to avoid being swept downstream as to avoid being killed by debris carried down by the current. These new backwaters also provide the fish with tempting new feeding grounds.

These areas are always worth a few casts, as they often hold surprisingly big fish. They are, however, invariably weedy, and fishing using conventional tackle is difficult. To keep your hook out of the weeds, use a buoyant bait on a simple flat-bottomed leger rig as shown.

Severe Flooding

Many anglers believe that fish die in winter because of the cold weather. Research has shown that far more deaths can be attributed to severe floods and the damage these waters can cause.

One important variable influencing the number of fish killed by floods is the presence of bankside vegetation in general, and trees in particular. Not only do trees provide food and cover for fish, but they also prevent the river from scouring during heavy floods.

During spring floods, many rivers break their banks and spread out onto the floodplains, flowing through the

Severe flooding, which is becoming more common in many areas, has a major impact on fish populations.

vegetation there. This reduces the pressure on the main channel and allows the greater volume of water to flow without causing too much damage to the river-bed and the fish living within it. In winter, however, snow can become compacted along the bank of a river that is devoid of thick vegetation. Under these circumstances, the banks are raised, and the depth of water flowing through them is increased. This can cause the bottom of the river to be scoured by the increased weight of water passing over it. Bottom-dwelling fish and invertebrates that can be swept away are killed, and rocks and debris lifted are carried downstream at speed toward any fish that are unlucky enough to be sitting in their path. In towns and cities, riverbanks are often built up artificially, and this can cause the same problems for fish. When trees and other bankside vegetation are present, the buildup of compacted snow is prevented, and the water can spill out over the banks at a lower stage of flood, reducing the scouring.

Flooding can cause losses of especially large numbers of young fish. Fry tend to gather in the margins and just below the surface along the main body of a river. When floodwater breaks the banks, it is these upper layers that are initially washed over the sides, and fry are stranded in the hundreds of thousands as a result.

Prey and Predation

In spite of the dangers that floods present, they also provide fish with substantial benefits. In addition to opening up new forage grounds, heavy rains wash huge numbers of insects and other terrestrials into lakes and rivers, where fish feed on them voraciously. Invertebrates commonly eaten include aphids, maggots, tree bugs, land beetles, wood lice, and spiders. Fish will take a slug more readily during a flood than under other conditions, suggesting that they are actually looking for them during high water levels. A cast into marginal backwaters with a slug or earthworm will often prove successful.

> **Tight Lines**
> During flooding, a cast into marginal backwaters with a slug or earthworm will often prove successful.

Floods also eliminate, either temporarily or permanently, some predators from the fish's environment. Snakes that feed on fish are unable to do so during severe flooding, and they are forced to take cover in the trees or on high ground. If you are in an area inhabited by venomous snakes, be very careful during floods, as they are likely to congregate in the same areas as people.

The North American river otter is an efficient predator of fish, but its young are at risk during severe flooding.

The young of fish-eating predators, such as the North American river otter, are commonly washed away during floods. As the rushing waters tear away the banks, young mammals nesting within them are separated from their parents and are often drowned or crushed.

Aquatic mammals and fish species often feed voraciously immediately after a flood because they may have been unable to feed for hours or even days of high, fast water. Furthermore, there is a bounty of carcasses readily available to any scavengers. These easy pickings make predators less likely to pursue surviving fish, which in turn are able to feed on the bounty of terrestrial invertebrates that have been washed into the water.

During such times, dead baits are likely to be effective, as predatory fish will be searching for casualties on the bottom, especially in eddies and backwaters where dead fish collect. A common mistake is to assume that all dead fish float. In fact, many dead fish initially sink to the bottom, where bacteria begin to feed on them and produce gases as a by-product of respiration. Only when the gases build up to a substantial volume, typically after a period of days, will dead fish float to the surface.

> **Tight Lines**
> Dead baits are likely to be effective after a flood, as predators search for casualties along the bottom.

Water Clarity

As discussed, turbidity describes the presence of suspended particles in the water column causing cloudiness and reducing visibility. It is most often caused by turbulence, which is a state of movement or agitation of the water. Generally speaking, rivers are more turbid than lakes, and coastal margins are more turbid than the open water.

A long period of fine weather can increase the visibility within a body of shallow water by as much as twenty times that immediately after a flood. (Turbulence also breaks up the surface water and reduces visibility from above.)

After a flood, fish are likely to scavenge on the bottom or feed just below the surface. One study examined the stomach contents of stickleback and found that turbidity was a key factor influencing feeding rates. Turbidity led some stickleback to feed closer to the surface, where light levels were stronger. In clear water, they detected prey up to a maximum distance of 44 centimeters, while in turbid water, this was reduced to 26 centimeters. Not surprisingly, the time taken to capture a prey item increased with turbidity.

After a flood, turbidity and turbulence provide prey fish with a "virtual weed bed" in which they are less visible to predators. This encourages them to leave cover and forage more freely in open water. To make the most of this when fly- or lure-fishing, use large flies or baits to enhance visibility—the more turbid the water, the larger the fly or bait should be. Use strong-smelling baits to exploit the fact that the fish

For anglers not wishing to use dead baits, realistic-looking replicas such as these perch can be very effective. These plastic replacements will not attract fish by smell, however, so they will not be very effective in turbid floodwaters.

Fish become stressed when drought reduces a river's flow and forces them into smaller habitats.

will be relying more heavily than usual on their other senses to make up for their inability to see as clearly.

Droughts

Droughts force fish into smaller areas, making locating and catching them less of a challenge. In the Northern Hemisphere, droughts occur most commonly during the months of July and August, while flooding occurs most commonly during the spring and winter. As climate change is widely anticipated to worsen, droughts will become more common in the future.

As the water levels recede, fish become stressed. This initially makes them more aggressive and prone to snap at brightly colored lures passing at speed. This can provide great sport, but it is short-lived. As water levels fall further, fish are driven into deeper pools, the larger fish being the first to be forced to move in, while smaller fish may remain in the very shallow streams as long as possible to avoid predation. When the fish congregate into pools, different tactics are required.

Riverine fish like trout have strong hierarchies, and once in the pools, these hierarchies often change. Food sources are limited within the pool, and competition for any morsel is intense. The dominant fish is commonly overthrown by another individual better adapted to life within the drought pool—perhaps one that is smaller but faster. While the biggest fish at the beginning of a drought may lose weight quickly, its successor is unlikely to become bigger than it was at the beginning of the drought, so over time, the fish living in the pool become more equal in size. Hunger-stressed fish naturally have a propensity to strike hastily, and the angler

Tight Lines
If you wish to catch the largest fish in the pool, it is crucial to fish as soon as the water level begins to drop.

can take advantage of this, but if you wish to catch the largest fish in the pool, it is crucial to fish as soon as the water level begins to drop and before the process of equalization begins.

Droughts are good times for predators, including many predatory fish species sought by anglers. As prey species are forced to share small pools with them, life becomes comparatively easy for species like northern pike, which can consume every fish around them. For the angler, this means that predatory fish are likely to be larger and in better fighting condition a few days after the waters have returned.

But anglers will face competition during droughts, too. So many fish trapped in a small pool creates ideal feeding conditions for predatory birds, including herons and kingfishers, and for mammals, such as otters.

Nevertheless, droughts are a good time to introduce newcomers to the sport, as the fish can be easily seen, and they are often easier to catch. Most baits will get a bite. Be aware, however, that if you can see the fish, they can see you. Approach the water with care so as not to spook the fish. Dress in dull-colored clothing and avoid especially bright yellow, which appears to be the worst color for concealment.

Once a drought-stressed fish has been scared, it may not feed for a long time. If you do spook the fish, it is often worth traveling to the next pool and starting again.

> **Tight Lines**
> Droughts are a good time to introduce newcomers to the sport, as the fish can be easily seen, and they are often easier to catch.

Ice

When ice forms on rivers and lakes, a number of new variables enter into the equation, and finding the right place to fish can become a challenge. Ice can affect water temperature, light levels, oxygen content, current speed, food sources, predation, shelter, and, of course, fishing tactics.

Ice Dams

Hanging ice dams are caused when surface ice develops in a region of relatively slow-flowing water. Ice particles washed downstream from faster waters float to the surface when the flow slows down and freeze onto the bottom of the existing surface ice. This process continues to thicken the ice dam until no more ice

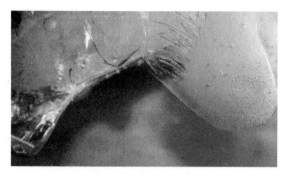

As surface ice forms and melts, its shape beneath the surface is carved by the water's flow.

> **Tight Lines**
> Large fish can often be found hiding just out of the flow channel.

Current

Ice dam

Fish lurk behind ice dams, collecting food as it flows through the narrowed channel.

particles are able to take hold for some reason—for example, if the temperature increases. An ice dam may also cease to thicken when it becomes so thick that it constricts the flow of water, causing the water to speed up as it passes through a smaller gap, thus preventing the ice particles from floating up to the underside of the ice dam and adhering to it.

Initially, these areas of faster flow channel food particles drifting downstream into a tight flow. Large fish can often be found hiding just out of the flow, gathering the particles as they pass. Under these conditions, it is often productive to fish in the slack water behind the ice dam. The open channels below dams are often fairly close to the riverbed, so it is worth fishing a weighted bait that will stay down and roll around within the slack water.

When ice dams become too large, fish will move away from them, as the flow rate may become too high for them to intercept food or hold their position in the water.

Icebergs

Icebergs—free-floating chunks of ice—present interesting opportunities to anglers. A study of the effects of bergs on the feeding behavior of river-dwelling trout observed that even in these freezing conditions, trout would swim between large ice blocks and examine food particles presented by the slow flow of the river. The trout avoided the ice masses themselves but were seen to feed on the river bottom around their edges. The researchers suggested that the movement of these large ice clumps by the water flow dislodged aquatic invertebrates hiding in the substrate, offering the trout a higher-than-normal quota of bottom-dwelling food. An abundance of aquatic invertebrate life actively crawling over the ice was also observed, and the study described how, although the trout were feeding actively around these icebergs, they were considerably slower in their movements than they had been when observed during the summer months. (In separate studies, trout have also been observed feeding on invertebrates crawling on the undersides of icebergs drifting down rivers.)

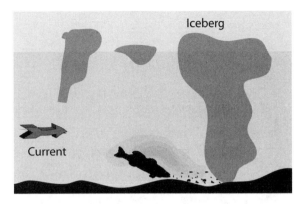

Some fish will follow drifting icebergs, feeding as the moving ice dislodges invertebrates from the bottom.

Trout gathering around the bases of these drifting bergs picking off any prey species thrown up by the ice are an ideal target for the winter angler. Using a weighted fly or bait just behind a drifting berg is likely to pick up a fish on the feed. Once again, try to fish as close to the riverbed as possible, as this is where the fish will be feeding.

This tactic only works if the berg is drifting slowly. If the berg is moving quickly or is accompanied by numerous pieces of broken ice, the fish will take cover, and different tactics will be required. This is explained in more detail later.

> ***Tight Lines***
> Use a weighted fly or bait to pick up trout gathered around an iceberg in search of prey species thrown up by the ice.

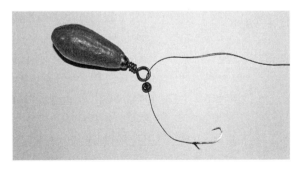

This rolling rig, a heavy leger rig, will ensure that the bait remains on or near the bottom. The round lead weight will also allow the bait to roll and move with the shifting ice.

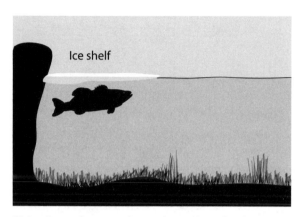

Fish often take cover beneath overhanging ice.

Ice Shelves

Ice shelves attached to the margins of rivers or lakes improve the habitat for fish in several respects. Because they protect fish from predatory birds, ice shelves represent a safe haven. When snow settles on the ice, it provides insulation, keeping the water below it slightly warmer. And as noted above, ice provides a habitat for invertebrates, and hence a food source for the fish that shelter there.

So beneficial is ice cover to fish that, when it melts early, experiments have shown that fish grow less and are less likely to survive. The longer the ice cover lasts, the bigger the fish grow. Obviously, these conditions are also good for anglers.

Tight Lines
Take note of the nature of the ice cover if you catch a good fish during the winter; try it again when you spot similar conditions elsewhere or next year.

Within any given environment, a fish will occupy the best possible position. It will look for a good source of food and adequate protection from predation. During winter, the configuration of ice shelves attached to the margins of bodies of water changes regularly. These expand at night, being at their largest as dawn approaches. As the ice changes, the area may become better or worse for fish, and as a result, they will move around. Because of their activity periods, this is most likely to be at night. For this reason, it is important to keep trying previously unsuccessful locations, and try to keep an eye on the changes in the ice. If you catch a good fish in a certain place, don't just remember the location; take a look at the nature of the ice cover and try it again when conditions are the same, either later in the winter or in subsequent years.

When the water becomes totally covered by surface ice, limited oxygen exchange occurs between the air and the water. If adequate light enters the water through the ice, aquatic plants will produce oxygen via photosynthesis. At night when the sunlight fades, the plants use up oxygen. Because temperatures are low, this process is very slow and in larger, sparsely weeded bodies of water is rarely a significant problem. Under most ice-cover conditions, the fish will remain in deeper water until the ice melts.

Various factors can conspire to reduce oxygen to problematic levels. This is especially the case during periods of prolonged ice cover and in smaller ponds. Oxygen levels may become low in the deeper water. Reduced mixing due to the lack of wind exposure can cause suspended debris in the water to fall to the bottom, where it is broken down by oxygen-consuming bacteria. Further deoxygenation can be caused if

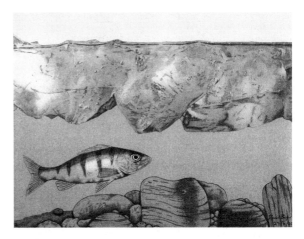

Ice cover can be important for fish survival but it can also cause problems.

aquatic plants are present and snow falls onto the ice, blocking out the sunlight. In these circumstances, the plants, unable to use the sunlight to produce oxygen, use up the oxygen reserves within the lake. Deoxygenation will be most severe at the bottom of a lake or river, and in extreme conditions, any fish trapped beneath the ice may asphyxiate. To avoid this, fish will congregate just beneath the ice where temperatures are lower and oxygen levels slightly higher, but this is only a short-term solution and will not sustain them for long. If you are breaking the ice for the first time to fish a small pond, try fishing at the surface and work your way down. Trout in particular are often found higher in the water column.

> **Tight Lines**
> Fish the surface and work your way down when breaking the ice for the first time in a small pond.

Ice Fishing

Ice fishing confers several advantages to the angler. It permits fishing anywhere on the lake without a boat and without having to cast long distances from the bank. The angler is well hidden from the fish. Ice fishing can provide a great variety of fish to catch. On larger lakes, there are likely to be a large diversity of species, including largemouth bass, trout, sunfish, chain pickerel, northern pike, muskellunge, crappie, yellow perch, and walleye. With all its benefits, it's surprising that more people don't try it. Here are a number of tips for successful ice fishing:

▶ A minimum thickness of 5 inches of ice should be observed. Because ice thickness on any body of water can be variable, be careful to check the thickness at regular intervals so that you do not stumble accidentally onto thin ice. A fall through the surface ice in these conditions can easily result in a fatality.

▶ Always go with a friend, so that one person can assist in a rescue or raise the alarm if an accident occurs.

▶ There are often restrictions on the number of holes you are able to fish at once, and you must always stay within sight of any line you have set so that you can pull the fish in when it takes the bait.

▶ One of the most important pieces of equipment when ice fishing is a map showing the underwater features of the pond or lake. If you are unable to get hold of one of these, it is well worth seeking advice from a fellow angler who has local knowledge. Unless you know what you are fishing over, you are losing one of the main advantages of ice fishing: the ability to choose the perfect location.

▶ The density of water is temperature dependent. Water is at its densest at 39.092°F (3.94°C). Water at this temperature sinks to the bottom of the lake when ice forms. For this reason, the deeper water near the lake bed is the warmest location. The water gets cooler closer to the surface, until it freezes just beneath the surface layer of ice. This provides a temperature buffer for those fish trapped beneath the ice and shelters them from the freezing weather above.

Once the hole has been bored into the ice, there are two main choices of tactics. One is a small hook baited with either a small bait like mealworms or heavily scented power bait. This rig will attract smaller fish species and is likely to produce a bite faster. The other option is a dead bait to attract larger fish like bass, northern pike, and walleye. With both methods, it is best to fish the bait just off the bottom, as this water is warmer and is the spot most likely to be where the fish are resting (although, as mentioned earlier, it is worth testing the surface water on the way down). Fish will be less active in cold conditions, so if you use lures or jigs, keep the movement down to a slow pace, allowing them plenty of time to see the bait and take a bite.

Fish will congregate around sunken roots, rocks, vegetation, and drop-offs, so use your map to identify submerged features and concentrate your efforts there. Where there are smaller fish, there will be larger predators waiting in ambush, so the same habitat is likely to be productive for both.

Dead baits are especially effective when fishing for northern pike. In these cold conditions, a strongly scented bait is very tempting, and very large specimens can be taken in this way. Make sure you use line of adequate strength, as you may catch something bigger than expected. If you are targeting predatory fish, use a metal leader (i.e., a trace) between your line and your hook. This thin wire ensures that the line will not be cut by the predator's sharp teeth as you pull it through the water.

Breakup

Large ice masses over rivers can move downstream during the breakup that comes with spring thaw or during other periods of high water discharge. If the ice mass is moving quickly or if there are large quantities of broken ice, the fish will seek refuge. Movements of the fish during these periods are generally in a downstream direction. They are simply forced along by the strong flow and the debris within it.

Throughout periods of high discharge and ice breakup, all fish spend significantly more time in backwater habitats. In many cases, the depth of these backwaters is greater than in the main stream, while the water velocity is often less, and these backwaters thus provide

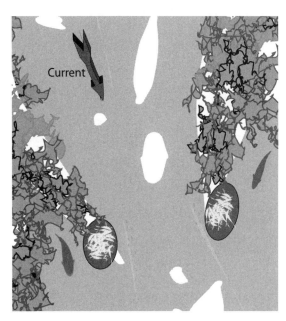

During ice breakup, fish seek refuge from chunks of ice being carried rapidly downstream.

an ideal shelter for fish. The raised water levels provide protection from predators and access to flooded food beds, while the slower flow rate reduces the amount of energy required to hold position and makes it easier to avoid any large pieces of broken ice that happen to move out of the main stream and into the backwater. Winter fish (especially salmon) often gather in great numbers in these areas, and under such conditions, time should not be wasted fishing the main channel.

> **Tight Lines**
> Winter fish often gather in great numbers in backwater areas.

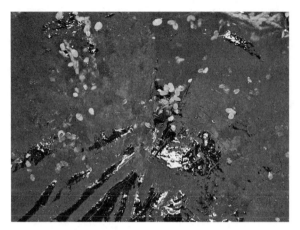

Surface ice breaking up.

The weed rig is created using a lead with a flat base that holds its ground without snagging and a buoyant float to ensure that the hook line and bait remain above the weeds on the bottom.

Remember that these newly flooded areas are often full of vegetation and snags. Use strong line, buoyant baits, and rigs that are designed for weedy places, such as the weed rig shown here.

Did Ice Lead to the Invention of the Fishing Rod?

It is interesting to speculate how weather has influenced fishing over the millennia. It is possible that ice played a crucial role in the invention of rod-and-line fishing as we know it.

The history of fishing by man goes back to our earliest human origins. Evolving in Africa, our ancestors found that spacious, storm-cut cave systems made ideal shelter, and an abundance of intertidal invertebrates and fish made for a ready food supply.

The migration from Africa to Europe around eight hundred thousand years ago was not a deliberate trip but an accident of population growth. As human numbers increased, so too did competition for food resources, and people moved along the coast to fresh pastures. As there were people living for miles behind them, there was only one direction in which they could move to find new, unexplored resources.

As humans migrated to northern Europe, they experienced much harsher winters. Spearfishing in icy conditions is very difficult, as the ice itself blocks the strike path of the spear. Exposed to these conditions, our ancestors could have used a rock to smash through the ice and waited for fish to pass before spearing them through the hole. These spear fishermen would have learned (perhaps by accident) that putting small quantities of food into the hole would attract fish, reducing the amount of time spent exposed to the harsh weather and the man-eating predators around at this time.

Did the obvious discomfort of this scene lead to the development of modern tackle?

Watching the fish swim past and grab the food offerings created a situation in which the intellectual leap from spear to hook does not seem so difficult. A piece of food was initially tied directly to a line made of gut or something similar. The first steps toward modern fishing had been taken. Eventually, real hooks would be fashioned of bone or wood, and then barbs added to increase their holding power. Since the hook might have floated up against the bottom of the ice cover, weights would have been added to make a better presentation.

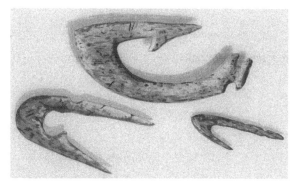

Early hooks made from wood and bone.

Early man would have been quick to notice another huge advantage of ice fishing with hook and line as opposed to a spear: baited hooks could be left unattended for hours at a time, permitting the fisherman to retreat into a warm, safe place while food gathering went on uninterrupted. It also enabled fishermen to set multiple traps, increasing the odds of taking a fish and increasing the take.

The addition of a rod would allow the line to be securely tied in place before being left. By tying the line to a longer pole, the line became easier to handle; it was now possible to cast the bait farther and into previously unreachable places; and the pole provided distance between the angler and the water, reducing the chances of spooking the fish.

CHAPTER **5**

Where the Fish Are in Their Underwater Habitats

As we have noted, fish tend to seek areas with the optimum combination of several variables, including the following:

- ▶ Temperature
- ▶ Light level
- ▶ Oxygen content
- ▶ Water level
- ▶ Cover
- ▶ Food supply
- ▶ Predation
- ▶ Water quality

The above list is as yet incomplete. This chapter looks into the influence of nutrient levels, flow and turbulence, pressure and depth, and cover on the habitat choices made by fish. Though some of these topics, like flow and turbulence, have already been mentioned or discussed in previous chapters, we will go into them in greater detail here. These factors come into play in almost every angling situation. By understanding what drives fish to move from one place to the next, it is possible to make sure that your hook is dropped in the right location.

Nutrient Levels

The nutrient levels present within any body of water drive the overall productivity of the ecosystem from the bottom of the chain (plants producing energy from the sun) right up to the top (the mammals and birds that are predators of fish). The nutrient levels of a lake are often governed by the surrounding geology. Water falls as rain onto land and then drains through the streams and rivers into ponds and lakes. If the water running into the lake flows over bare rock, then it will not absorb many nutrients. If, on the other hand, the lake is surrounded by fertile farmland, then the water will collect nutrients on its way into the lake.

Lakes can be categorized according to the nutrients that feed into them. *Oligotrophic* lakes have a poor supply of nutrients. This leads to a low rate of formation of organic matter by photosynthesis, as the plants do not have adequate nutrients to proliferate. The lack of plant life leads to a lack of invertebrate life, which in turn limits the number of fish that are able to survive within that body of water.

Eutrophic lakes are those containing high levels of nutrients that in turn promote an abundance of plant life, feeding large numbers of invertebrates. A eutrophic lake can support a large number of fish. In between oligotrophic and eutrophic lakes are the *mesotrophic* lakes, with moderate nutrient levels that can support a moderate population of fish.

Oligotrophic lakes are characterized by clear waters and little vegetation along the margins. Eutrophic lakes have colored water and plenty of visible vegetation. It is important for anglers to be aware of these distinctions, as they dramatically influence the types and numbers of fish present within the lake. Eutrophic lakes have a comparatively wide diversity of fish species living within them as well as larger populations. Oligotrophic lakes have fewer species of fish and smaller populations. (It is also important to distinguish between naturally eutrophic lakes and lakes that have suffered from excessive artificially induced *eutrophication*, in which high levels of nutrients entering a lake in the form of sewage or fertilizers lead to a huge and rapid growth of algae, known as an "algal bloom." As the algae naturally dies, it is broken down by bacteria that consume oxygen. This can cause oxygen levels within the water body to crash. This leads to large-scale kills of fish and other aquatic organisms, whose decomposition further reduces oxygen levels.)

Given the general superiority of the fishing in eutrophic lakes, it would seem that there would be little point in fishing an oligotrophic lake if given the choice. Oligotrophic lakes may, however, contain one of the most sought-after game fish of all, the ferox trout. This is a common brown trout that has been forced to become a cannibal due to a limited food supply in its home waters. Once these big trout begin feeding on smaller trout, they can grow to huge sizes. Part of the mystique of the ferox trout comes from the fact that they live in such wild places, and the small fish populations in these waters require that the angler have a high level of skill (or a huge amount of luck) to hunt them down. Waters like the infamous Loch Ness and Loch Awe of Scotland are classic oligotrophic lakes where ferox trout are found. These waters tend to be big, and finding even big trout in such a vast expanse is a real test of an angler's ability to read the weather, pinpoint exactly where the fish are likely to be, determine when they are likely to be feeding, and decide what to use in the way of bait, lure, or fly to tempt them.

Water Flow

Peregrine falcons are the fastest animals on the planet. These birds are excellent fliers and are experts at using the wind to their advantage. They actually prefer hunting in strong winds, as this gives them the edge when chasing less agile prey species.

The peregrine's wind is the fish's water, and in the same way, some fish are better adapted to stronger currents than others. Animals have evolved to fit into certain biological niches, adapting themselves to living among particular plants and animals as well as evolving the ability to make allies of certain environmental conditions.

The maximum swimming speeds of different freshwater fish are related closely to the flow of water in the areas they inhabit. Salmon, for example, can swim at 800 centimeters per second; trout at 400 centimeters per second; chub at 270 centimeters per second; bream at 55 to 65 centimeters per second; pike at 45 centimeters per second; and carp at 40 centimeters per second. Most species are

Fast-flowing water represents a significant barrier to some fish species and an ideal habitat to others.

associated with particular flow zones within any given river. Salmon, for example, tend to live in the faster-flowing, shallow, upland waters, while carp dominate the deep, comparatively slow, lowland stretches.

Just because a fish can swim fast doesn't mean it likes to spend its time in the fast flow. An interesting experiment using a simulated river to study how flow rate influences where salmon can be found showed that the faster the water flow, the greater the rate of downstream emigration. The researchers noted that when the flow increased even only slightly, the salmon were more likely to migrate into the slack water habitats at the margins of the river. Even the highest flow rates were still well below the maximum swimming speeds of the fish. This suggests that the fish *chose* to move away as the flow increased to conserve energy and were not simply washed downstream.

Flow and Feeding

Another study focused on the influence of flowing and still water on the feeding behavior of Atlantic salmon. The study found that young salmonids only fed on food items that were in motion. The salmon darted at prey approaching them from the front but did not consume stationary prey items. They were never seen to be searching for food. Instead, they would remain in one place and wait for the current to bring the food to them.

The same study found that water fleas (tiny crustaceans) were consumed by the salmon in still water. The researchers also found that if a salmon disturbed the sediment, it would then feed on the particles brought into suspension. They concluded that prey movement was enough to elicit feeding in still water. Movement need not be great in order for it to induce a feeding response. Mayfly nymphs were scattered onto the bottom of an aquarium containing salmon and trout. Half of the mayflies were dead and half were alive. The living mayflies remained still, and the only difference between them and the dead ones was the intermittent vibrations of their delicate, minute gill structures called *lamellae*. The living nymphs were rapidly attacked and eaten, and the dead ones were all ignored. It was concluded that salmon are able to feed successfully in still water, provided they are regularly exposed to moving prey. So keep your flies twitching.

Flow, Shelter, and Schooling

Man has built many structures that alter the flow within rivers: these include dams, fish ladders, bridges, canals, bank protection of various types, docks and piers, reservoirs, and more. Rivers passing through cities have been the most heavily modified, especially by canalization and hard bank protection, and these stretches are subject to the most extreme changes in water levels and flow rates. Because the water has nowhere else to go, they are particularly prone to flash flooding.

Flow is one of the most important factors influencing a river and the fish that inhabit it. A natural watercourse is much more able to buffer environmental changes and maintain steadier rates of flow, and when water levels rise, new areas of refuge often open up for fish. In contrast, heavily engineered stretches often lack suitable habitat for fish to hide behind even under relatively benign conditions of flow and so tend to contain fewer fish.

When schools of game fish move through areas of fast flow, they are likely to break up into smaller groups. These groups will contain fish of similar sizes: the smaller fish will gather together into one group, and the larger fish will form another group. This segregation is based on strength and speed. If there is a good source of food at the head of a fast-flowing stretch, the larger game fish will monopolize this area. They are better able to both maintain position and resist competition from their smaller school mates. Another aspect of schooling by size is predator avoidance. Larger fish are naturally more attractive to many predators, but when large fish all gather together, no one fish stands out as particularly appealing prey.

In areas with rich feeding grounds and in fisheries with a high stock density, size groups tend to mix together more readily. If you are casting to a school, always cast to the front. This will yield better results, as all of the fish will pass over the bait.

Remember that on enclosed still waters, current is driven by the wind. (See Chapter 3.) The surface water moves in the same direction as the wind, while beneath the surface, a compensating current travels in the opposite direction. This is very useful to consider when approaching a larger fish at depth in clear water. Keep in mind that the direction of the current at the depth of the fish may not be the same as that on the surface.

> **Tight Lines**
> When fishing around underwater features keep an eye on the flow. If the current is fast, use a weight to drop the bait onto the bottom. If it is slow, keep the bait higher in the water.

When fishing around underwater features such as submerged islands, be aware of the current. Fish congregating around features stay higher in the water column at lower flow rates and sink deeper, remaining closer to the ground or feature, as flow increases. If the current is fast, use a weight to drop the bait onto the bottom. If it is slow, keep the bait higher in the water.

When river fishing, remember that the flow velocity is greatest in the middle of the stream and slower at the edges due to friction caused by the riverbed, submerged plants, and debris. Always gauge the flow speed by observing the area you are going to fish, and work the midstream area or the banks accordingly.

Confluences

The "best" positions hold the biggest fish. These are the positions that require the least energy to hold (remain relatively still) in, such as behind a large boulder or tree root, and where a good flow of water brings plenty of food into reach. Once a fish is removed from or leaves such a position, it will be quickly replaced by another.

In a confluence, where two rivers meet and the flows collide, an area of turbulent water is created. This turbulent water is fronted by a land mass that creates an eddy. For fish, this is an ideal place to live because, in addition to being able to shelter from the current, they have the benefit of two rivers moving twice as much food past their hiding place. The turbulence in these spots also oxygenates the water and provides cover from predators. These areas are often home to large individuals or large numbers of smaller fish, depending on the species. For territorial fish like brown trout and pike, there will be one large individual. For communal species like carp, many fish will gather in a school.

Current

Current

Fish often congregate where two rivers meet.

> **Tight Lines**
> Where two rivers meet is a great place to catch fish.

Heads of Pools and Riffle Beds

Water passing through the bottleneck at the head of a pool speeds up and mixes with the surrounding air, becoming rich in oxygen. Food flowing within the stream or river often provides the main food source in the pool, and the bottleneck funnels that food into a narrow, shallow area that can be easily scanned by

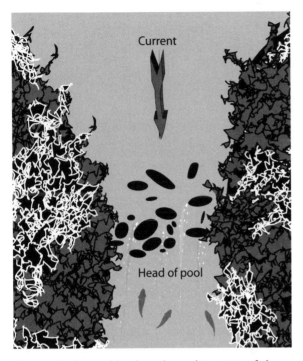

Current

Head of pool

The head of a pool is often the main source of the resident fishes' food.

fish. About the only drawback from the fish's point of view is that the shallow water exposes it to predation. Consequently, fish often feed in these areas under the relative cover of dawn and dusk. When fishing the head of a pool, drop a natural bait or imitation into the flow upstream of the head during twilight hours. The bait will roll naturally with the flow through the bottleneck, where it will likely be snatched up by a feeding fish.

Riffle beds are raised areas of riverbed that cause the water's velocity to increase, thus creating a comparatively oxygen-rich stretch. Trout spawn in these areas, and many adult fish stay here long after the spawning season has ended.

Trout living in fast-flowing water have to use more energy to hold their position. These fish grow more slowly and mature at an older age, and they are often smaller than those found in slow-flowing, deeper swims.

Fish can be washed downstream if the flow is too high, and rivers with lower flows show higher survival rates of trout fry than those with higher flows. There are likely to be more fry surviving in and around slower-flowing riffle beds, and fishing downstream of such places can lead to pools holding trout. The larger fish remain in the territory nearest to the spawning grounds, while smaller fish are displaced downstream until the fish population is reduced enough so they can establish their own territory.

Being territorial, trout aggressively fend off other fish. Studies have shown that the more rocks on a riverbed, the more territories trout will establish. Being visually screened from each other allows the fish to feel secure in smaller territories that are in closer proximity. The lesson is obvious:

Tight Lines
Seek places with plenty of large boulders, as they will likely hold a greater number of fish.

seek places with plenty of large boulders, as they will likely hold a greater number of fish.

Trout tend to cling to the bottom of a river or stream using their pectoral fins during periods of especially high flow. Any fly or bait used in very high flows should therefore be heavily weighted to bring it down to the fish on the riverbed.

Grayling prefer to spend the summer months in faster-flowing water over cobble boulder, where they can be found in the margins. During the autumn, they move to slower-flowing water over sandy areas and can be found midchannel.

Turbulence

Turbulence and water flow are inextricably connected. Where we dealt primarily with water speed and shelter in the previous section, here we will focus on visual cover and the oxygenating effects of these interconnected phenomena.

Turbulence can be caused by the physical terrain over which the water is flowing. On riffle beds, friction between the water and the gravel beds and rocks over which it passes causes the surface to break and become turbulent. When water passes over large obstacles, it is pushed up to the surface. This water then trails behind the object, providing turbulent cover.

Weather conditions can also mix up the surface waters. The pounding effect of raindrops, especially during heavy rain, and the friction of the wind pulling past the surface cause flat water to break up, creating an area of turbulence.

A river's physical terrain can change its flow, infuencing where fish are likely to be hiding.

Visual Impact

Turbulence significantly impairs the view of the underwater world from above. It is for this reason that fountains are recommended as deterrents to fish-eating birds in garden koi ponds.

In the absence of weed cover or cloudy water, turbulence is sought by fish seeking shelter from predators. In small chalk streams and rivers, surface turbulence can account for almost all of the visual cover available to resident fish. Trout, especially, will spend the day just below turbulent surface waters.

Turbulence and Oxygen

Tight Lines
In a reservoir, the aeration vents can provide an excellent place to fish.

When oxygen levels are low, fish are attracted to areas of higher oxygen content. This is especially the case during the low water levels of a drought. The water falling over a waterfall or passing through a man-made fountain mixes with the highly oxygenated air, providing an oxygen-rich area for fish.

In a reservoir, the aeration vents can provide an excellent place to fish. Fish are attracted in great numbers by the higher oxygen levels and the turbulence that stirs up food and gathers it into food lanes.

Use a colorful bait, fly, or lure in these turbulent environments. Although fish will take more drab baits, the high flow will stir up sediment, and the whitewater itself will limit the fish's vision. The brighter the fly, the more likely it is to be seen. For this reason, bait presentation is also less important. Fish in these highly oxy-

Waterfalls provide fish with oxygen-rich, well-covered feeding grounds.

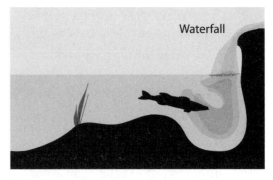

Fish frequently gather at the base of a waterfall, which often scours out an area of relatively deep water.

genated areas are likely to take vigorously. Be ready to strike, and make sure your line is of adequate strength.

When there is no oxygenating water feature, fish will move into weedy areas at dusk and gasp beneath the surface. In deeper water on hot days, the fish tend to hide away in the deeper areas where oxygen levels are more comfortable.

Pollution can significantly reduce oxygen levels within water. Although fish will usually avoid polluted areas, in some cases, worryingly, fish react positively to pollutants, actively seeking them out and, once surrounded by them, refusing to reenter pure water. It is possible that the pollutants stimulate the fish in some way, as many toxins do to humans (alcohol, for example). Whether the fish are enjoying themselves or not, there is no doubt that these chemicals are harmful to them. High levels of pollution will in most cases kill any fish that are unable to escape.

Fishing Turbulent Waters

Moderate levels of movement in the water increase the encounter rates between fish and their food. Areas in which this is common, such as lake margins on windy days and pools below dams, are often filled with foraging fish.

If the level of turbulence becomes too intense, however, the fish will be unable to catch their prey, and these areas will lose their appeal. In particularly turbid waters, fish will pull back and can often be found waiting in slacker water nearby for any food items to be thrown out by the turbulence.

When fishing turbulent water, do not weight the bait or fly down too much. It must be light enough to move naturally so that it will eventually pass into the calmer water and in front of the waiting fish. If it is too heavy, it will simply sink to the bottom of the turbulent flow and not be found.

> **Tight Lines**
> When fishing turbulent water, do not weight the bait or fly down too much.

Depth

A fish's depth within the water column is, in part, determined by the available food supply. For both river- and lake-dwelling trout, the main bulk of their diet consists of organisms living at or near the bottom. In some streams, however, a comparative lack of *benthic* (i.e., bottom-dwelling) organisms or an abundance of fly life can lead to an increase in the importance of surface feeding.

Terrestrial insects, like this grasshopper lurking in marginal vegetation, represent an important food source in some water bodies.

There is a greater number of insects per unit area in rivers than in lakes, and greater insect diversity. In rivers, the different emergence times of the various insect species are spread over a longer period, meaning food is available at the surface over more of the year.

The number of terrestrial insects taken from the surface varies considerably. In waters with a rich benthic fauna, terrestrials are rarely taken. In places with a shortage of bottom-dwelling prey items, terrestrials such as grasshoppers, ants, beetles, and inchworms play an important role in fishes' diets.

As trout get older, they feed more and more on benthic organisms. If you are looking to catch larger lake trout, then a dry fly is perhaps not the best approach. This is not to say that large lake trout do not consume flies on the surface, but research shows that smaller fish do so more readily.

> **Tight Lines**
>
> If you are looking to catch larger lake trout, then a dry fly is perhaps not the best approach.

Trout consume a greater number of terrestrial organisms than salmon. When exposed to different food sources, trout spend more of their time at different depths, making the most of the variety of food available.

Be aware of how changes in the weather may influence a fish's chosen depth. As discussed earlier, fish are likely to be in deeper water during winter and summer, as they take shelter from extreme temperatures. Trout will cease to feed on their normal aquatic food items during flooding, when caterpillars, earthworms, and slugs are washed into the water. At such times, fish terrestrials near the surface or in the margins.

Predation pressures will drive fish away from a preferred location into the relative safety of another area. If, for example, there are lots of predatory fish in one lake and not many predatory birds, the fish will spend most of their time in the shallows and away from the jaws of their predators. If the situation is reversed, then the fish will more often be found in deeper water. If there are large numbers of both birds and predatory fish, the prey fish will be hiding in weed cover or right up in the margins, under overhanging banks or trees.

It is reasonable to make generalizations about different species' preferences for different depths, as shown in this table, but this must be taken with a word of caution: the preference for depth is not only species-specific and weather-dependent but can also differ from population to population. The same species of fish in one river can behave in a different way to those in another. As I've urged before, local advice is often the best source of information.

Depth Preferences of Some Common Game Fish

Species	Depth Preference
Green sunfish, muskellunge, pumpkinseed, largemouth bass, bluegill, arctic grayling, flier, warmouth, white perch, pickerel	Shallow
Flathead catfish, spotted bass, cisco (i.e., lake herring), lake whitefish, sauger, yellow bullhead	Deep
Chinook salmon, coho salmon, cutthroat trout, rainbow trout, brown trout, brook trout	Deeper pools for shelter from temperature extremes; will venture into shallow water when conditions are suitable

When fishing at depth, use large flies or baits for better visibility. In shallow water where light penetrates easily, go smaller.

Fish tend to find their food either in the surface film, on the lake or river bed, or in the margins. The middle depths tend to be an unproductive "dead zone" because there is little food for fish there and no cover. It is always best to begin fishing either deep on the bottom or at the surface when fishing open water, and if you don't have quick success, work your way up or down until you find the fish.

Middle depths away from structure and shelter are often "dead zones" with comparatively few fish in residence.

The best way to accomplish this is to use a heavy bait or fly and vary the retrieve speed. The bait will sink quickly, but if you pull it back at a faster speed on each cast, it will have less time to sink. In this manner, the whole water column can be covered. Once the fish begin to bite, repeat the time the bait was left after the cast before the retrieve began and pull it in at the same speed. If the fish stop biting, start at the bottom again and work your way back up.

Visibility and Shelter

Fish living in shallow water are often camouflaged against the background, blending into their surroundings to avoid predatory birds and mammals. Those in deeper water are also camouflaged, but this tends to be less detailed or habitat-specific. These fish are often dark along the back to blend into the depths when seen from above and light on the underside to blend into the sky when seen from below.

In addition to these *physical* traits, fish pursue a variety of *behavioral* strategies to avoid being seen by predators or to hide from their prey until it is time to attack. In many cases, these are the primary factors leading to the selection of a habitat such as a shallow weed bed, an underwater feature like a log or a wreck, or an overhanging stream bank. In other situations, the availability of food or protection from bright sunlight may also influence the fish's choice.

Fish have a huge number of predators, and most of these hunt by sight. They have therefore evolved an instinct of shying away from environments that expose them to sight hunting. Very clear water is a dangerous place for a fish to spend its time and, given the choice, most species of fish will generally seek cover.

Overhanging Trees and Marginal Vegetation

Tight Lines
Where there are no deep pools, the fish will almost always be found under the nearest vegetation.

On hot, sunny days, fish congregate in shady areas to protect their eyes from the sun's direct glare and to seek cover from predators. Overhanging trees also provide food in the form of insects and other terrestrials. In waters where trees are absent, fish will be found hiding in the marginal vegetation.

Anglers commonly cast over the areas containing the most fish, in an attempt to reach the open water. If there are

In shallow, clear rivers, bankside cover is vital for fish.

deep pools and the sun is bright, the fish are indeed likely to seek cover there. But where there are no deep pools, the fish will almost always be found under the nearest vegetation.

Certain species of fish, such as trout, are especially dependent on cover, to the extent that their behavior is strongly influenced by its presence. One study found that trout could be positioned anywhere within an otherwise bare tank by providing the scantiest of cover. A square made from black insulating tape was placed on the floor of

This picture of a dried-up riverbed shows just how much cover the roots of overhanging trees can provide.

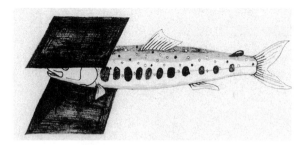

Researchers found that a trout would always place its head between the dark surfaces in an instinctive attempt to shelter from predators. When the water in the tank was given a directional flow, the fish remained "hidden" in this way but always pointed its head into the current.

an aquarium, and a second square was suspended in the water at a sufficient height above the first to allow the fish to place its head between them. With current flowing through the tank, the fish would always position themselves between the squares with their heads facing into the current and spent over 90 percent of their time in this position, regardless of where the "cover" was placed in the tank.

Projecting Structures

Where a stream has carved through bankside rock over the generations, the pools that are created may be obscured from above. These features provide the same service to fish as overhanging trees, and fish will congregate there seeking shade and protection from predators. Wherever you see rock jutting out close to the water's surface, it is always worth a try, as it may well hold a good fish. This is particularly the case during daylight hours. When night falls, the fish is likely to make the most of the cover of darkness and explore shallow, more exposed feeding grounds within its territory.

Where a river cuts through a muddy bank, roots of bankside vegetation and trees will often hold the surface layers together and lead to undercutting. Here the

Overhanging banks often shelter fish.

A brown trout takes cover under a rock.

mud below a bank is cut away by the flowing water creating an overhang. These areas are ideal for fish, as they have cover from light and predators as well as a food source from the invertebrates living within the soil.

Underwater Features

Fish love to feed around submerged islands and underwater features. These provide an abundance of food, cover from the elements, and protection from predators. Underwater structures can be shipwrecks, boulders, trees, and submerged man-made structures or even submerged islands (especially in reservoirs). All of these provide similar functions for fish.

When fishing these areas, use slightly heavier line. Submerged islands are weedy, and wrecks and rocky outcrops can snag and cut line easily. The fish's first instinct when hooked is to run for cover, and strong line will be required to get it out again. It is far better to keep the fish in open water where a line break is much less likely, and this requires being particularly vigilant to maintain a tight line at all times from the moment of hooking up.

Submerged islands are good places to find fish when the weather is calm, but the situation only gets better when the wind is blowing hard. Water movement stirs up shallow sediments, releasing food items and making the water cloudy. It is well worth taking a boat out and anchoring alongside one of these fishing hot spots. Use baits or imitations that resemble the invertebrate life stirred up from its hiding place within the shallow sediments and plants. This can be done by sampling

Fish are attracted to underwater features such as stumps, rocks, and wrecks, where they find cover and food.

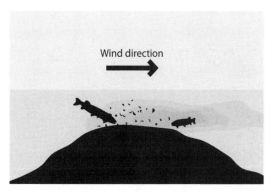

Subsurface islands are stirred up during stormy weather, which can expose food and attract fish.

the stomach contents of a fish that has been caught there or finding out from local anglers what the fish are likely to be feeding on.

As we have seen, fish are much more capable than most people believe. They react in diverse and complex ways to subtle changes within their world. I hope that this book has left you with a greater understanding of the causes of such behavioral changes and a deeper respect for the fish that you are trying to catch.

Chapter 1

6 **"One experiment done in 1984 clearly highlights the importance of the principle of energy conservation to anglers."** Fausch, K. D. (1984). Profitable stream positions for salmonids: relating specific growth rate to net energy gain. *Canadian Journal of Zoology* 62: 441–51.

Fausch studied positions held by salmonids within a stream. He built an aquarium that had two curves representing the typical shape of a stream. By pumping water through the tank and then back to a filter for cleaning before being pumped out again, he created an artificial stream. He placed stones in strategic positions and manipulated the sediment to create various types of microhabitat. The fins of the fish were clipped, allowing Fausch to identify individuals. Once the fish were introduced, their behavior was observed. Fausch conducted six experiments using coho salmon and brown and brook trout. One difference between the three species was that while the brown and brook trout used their pectoral fins to grip the bottom of the tank during periods of high water velocity, the coho salmon never rested on the bottom at any point. Fausch noted that the subordinate trout would hide, lodging themselves between the Plexiglas stream wall and the gravel. The dominant fish in all species would consistently retain the most profitable positions within the stream. Growth rates for these fish corresponded to their positions. Those in the best positions—that is, the ones requiring less energy (behind stones, for example) and with the best food supply (close to a fast current)—grew the fastest. The others were forced to take up lesser positions, and some fish were forced to settle for positions in which they actually lost weight. Oddly, Fausch described how during the experiment several of these fish took refuge in the gravel. All of those that did were never found by Fausch. They seemed to disappear when they swam beneath into the rocks, and he never saw them again.

22 "The most famous example of this is Niko Tinbergen's description of the reaction of his stickleback..." Kruuk, H. & Tinbergen, N. (2003). *Niko's Nature: A Life of Niko Tinbergen and His Science of Animal Behaviour.* Oxford: Oxford University Press, 87.

23 "In her excellent book *Through Our Eyes Only?*, Marian Stamp Dawkins..." Dawkins, M. S. (1998). *Through Our Eyes Only? The Search for Animal Consciousness.* Oxford: Oxford University Press.

24 "Experiments have shown that visual contrast is another vital factor both for predators and for prey." Cobcroft, J. M., Pankhurst, P. M., Hart, P. R. & Battaglene, S. C. (2001). The effects of light intensity and algae-induced turbidity on feeding behaviour of larval striped trumpeter. *Journal of Fish Biology* 59(5): 1181–97.

Cobcroft, Pankhurst, Hart, and Battaglene looked at the effects of turbidity on the feeding behavior of fish. They found increased feeding performance in turbid water and noted that reduced light intensity was not the cause. The enhanced feeding rates were the result of the increased contrast between the prey item and the background. This could occur as the light was scattered by the particles in the water.

26 "An intesting observation was made in 1965..." Phillips, C. (1965). *The Captive Sea: Fabulous Stories of Marine Life in One of the World's Greatest Seaquariums.* London: Frederick Muller Limited.

27 "Research has found that fish are vocal animals..." Bass, A. H. & McKibben, J. R. (2003). Neural mechanisms and behaviors for acoustic communication in teleost fish. *Progress in Neurobiology* 69(1): 1–26.

27 "Karl von Frisch changed that in the 1930s with an experiment that involved..." Von Frisch, K. (1938). The sense of hearing in fish. *Nature* 141: 8–11.

28 "Such experiments have determined that most fish have good hearing..." Tavolga, W. N., Popper, A. N. & Fay, R. J., eds. (1981). *Hearing and Sound Communication in Fishes.* New York: Springer-Verlag, 455.

37 "Von Frisch made an accidental discovery when one of his minnows was injured..." Von Frisch, K. (1938). Zur psychologie des fisch-schwarmes. *Die Naturwissenschaften* 26(37): 601–6.

Von Frisch, K. (1941). Über einen Schreckstoff der Fischhaut und seine biologische Bedeutung. *Zeitschrift für Vergleichende Physiologie* 29: 46–145.

38 **"Research has shown that trout have club cells . . ."** Scott, G. R., Sloman, K. A., Rouleau, C. & Wood, C. M. (2003). Cadmium disrupts behavioural and physiological responses to alarm substance in juvenile rainbow trout (*Oncorhynchus mykiss*). *Journal of Experimental Biology* 206: 1779–90.

38 **"In experiments, a large number of fish species have been tested for their taste response . . ."** One example: Valentinčič, T. & Caprio, J. (1997). Visual and chemical release of feeding behavior in adult rainbow trout. *Chemical Senses* 22(4): 375–82.

39 **". . . an experiment carried out by J. M. Elliott in 1975 on brown trout found that . . ."** Elliott, J. M. (1975). Weight of food and time required to satiate brown trout, *Salmo trutta* L. *Freshwater Biology* 5(1): 51–64.

39 **"A further paper by Elliott in the same year provided evidence that . . ."** Elliott, J. M. (1975). Number of meals in a day, maximum weight of food consumed in a day and maximum rate of feeding for brown trout, *Salmo trutta* L. *Freshwater Biology* 5(3): 287–303.

40 **"Recent studies have found that fish have abilities similar to nonhuman primates."** Brown, C., Dunbar, R., Kacelnik, A., Kendrick, K., Gosling, S., Else, L. & Douglas, K. (2004). Animal minds: do animals have minds of their own, and if they do, what might they be like? *New Scientist*, 12 June.

40 **"New research even credits fish with the human qualities of . . ."** Brown, C., Laland, K. & Krause, J., eds. (2006). *Fish Cognition and Behavior*. Cambridge: Blackwell Publishing.

41 **"Researchers filmed a male performing a courtship dance to females."** Rosenthal, G. G., Evans, C. S. & Miller, W. L. (1996). Female preference for dynamic traits in the green swordtail, *Xiphophorus helleri*. *Animal Behaviour* 51(4): 811–20.

41 **"Other researchers sped up the tapes and found that . . ."** Rowland, W. J. (1995). Do female stickleback care about male courtship vigour? Manipulation of display tempo using video playback. *Behaviour* 132(13–14): 951–61.

41 **"In another series of tests, scientists created dummies to represent female stickleback . . ."** Rowland, W. J. (1989). Mate choice and the supernormality effect in female sticklebacks (*Gasterosteus aculeatus*). *Behavioral Ecology and Sociobiology* 24(6): 433–38.

41 **"In similar experiments, female stickleback preferred the largest males."** Rowland, W. J. (1989b). The effects of body size, aggression, and nuptial col-

oration on competition for territories in male threespine sticklebacks, *Gasterosteus aculeatus. Animal Behaviour* 37(2): 282–89.

42 **"Studies suggest that fish are able to recognize the facial features of predators."** Helfman, G. S. (1989). Threat-sensitive predator avoidance in damselfish-trumpetfish interactions. *Behavioral Ecology and Sociobiology* 24(1): 47–58.

43 **"Scientists have found that when the tide is in, the gobies . . ."** Aronson, L. R. (1971). Further studies on orientation and jumping behavior in the gobiid fish, *Bathygobius soporator. Annals of the New York Academy of Sciences* 188: 378–92.

43 **"Experimenters provided rainbow trout with a lever . . ."** Boujard, T. & Leatherland, J. F. (1992). Demand-feeding behaviour and diel pattern of feeding activity in *Oncorhynchus mykiss* held under different photoperiod regimes. *Journal of Fish Biology* 40(4): 535–44.

44 **". . . researchers have also shown that fish prefer to be around those that are good at spotting predators."** Magurran, A. E., Oulton, W. J. & Pitcher, T. J. (1985). Vigilant behaviour and shoal size in minnows. *Zeitschrift für Tierpsychologie* 67(1–4): 167–78.

   Pitcher, T. J. & House, A. C. (1987). Foraging rules for group feeders: area copying depends upon food density in shoaling goldfish. *Ethology* 76(2): 161–67.

44 **"Perhaps the most interesting research yet undertaken provides insights into the personalities of fish."** Ward, G. & FitzGerald, G. J. (1987). Male aggression and female mate choice in the threespine stickleback, *Gasterosteus aculeatus. Journal of Fish Biology* 30(6): 679–90.

45 **"The latest research is even crediting fish with something that . . ."** Brown, C., Dunbar, R., Kacelnik, A., Kendrick, K., Gosling, S., Else, L. & Douglas, K. (2004). Animal minds: do animals have minds of their own, and if they do, what might they be like? *New Scientist* 12 June.

46 **"One study found that trout from fish farms removed from the water and exposed to the air . . ."** Kestin, S. (1997). Welfare of fish at slaughter. *Trout News.* Publication of the Centre for Environment, Fisheries & Aquaculture Science. 24: 42–44.

Chapter 2

51 "An experiment was designed to discover the effect a gradient in light intensity . . ." McNicol, R. E., Bégout-Anras, M. L. & Scherer, E. (1999). Influence of light preferences on the avoidance responses of lake whitefish, *Coregonus clupeaformis*, to cadmium. *Environmental Biology of Fishes* 55(3): 295–306.

54 "Another was shown in an experiment with rainbow trout that provides a glimpse into the influence light has on their feeding behavior." Boujard, T. & Leatherland, J. F. (1992). Demand-feeding behaviour and diel pattern of feeding activity in *Oncorhynchus mykiss* held under different photoperiod regimes. *Journal of Fish Biology* 40(4): 535–44.

56 "One study of the activity of stream-dwelling adult brown trout . . ." Young, M. K. (1999). Summer diel activity and movement of adult brown trout in high-elevation streams in Wyoming, U.S.A. *Journal of Fish Biology* 54: 181–89.

57 "The scientist F. R. Harden Jones observed some interesting changes in fish behavior with falling light levels." Harden Jones, F. R. (1956). The behaviour of minnows in relation to light intensity. *Journal of Experimental Biology* 33: 271–81.

58 "Scientific analysis of shark attacks on humans have shown that they peak twice a day . . ." Allen, T. B. (2001). *Shark Attacks: Their Causes and Avoidance.* New York: The Lyons Press, 44, 114 & 169.

59–60 "An early experiment provides valuable insight into just how aggressively fish react to reduced oxygen levels." Erichsen Jones, J. R. (1952). The reactions of fish to water of low oxygen concentration. *Journal of Experimental Biology* 29: 403–16.

64 "A study of the amount of time that trout required to digest food . . ." Elliott, J. M. (1972). Rates of gastric evacuation in brown trout *Salmo trutta* L. *Freshwater Biology* 2(1): 1–18.

65 "Years later, the study was expanded, and it was found that the appetite of brown trout varied with temperature." Elliott, J. M. (1975). Weight of food and time required to satiate brown trout, *Salmo trutta* L. *Freshwater Biology* 5(1): 51–64.

Elliott, J. M. (1975). Number of meals in a day, maximum weight of food consumed in a day and maximum rate of feeding for brown trout, *Salmo trutta* L. *Freshwater Biology* 5(3): 287–303.

Chapter 3

72   **"There is some evidence that certain species of fish are more active at higher wind speeds."** Lagardère, J.-P., Bégout, M.-L., Lafaye, J. Y. & Villotte J.-P. (1994). Influence of wind-produced noise on orientation in the sole (*Solea solea*). *Canadian Journal of Fisheries and Aquatic Sciences* 51(6): 1258–64.

       Lagardère, Bégout, Lafaye, and Villotte studied the influence of wind on the orientation of sole (*Solea solea*). They chose this species because its swimming activity occurred during the hours of darkness, and this meant that the fish were not relying on visual cues. During the experiment, meteorological and hydrological fluctuations were recorded. The fish were placed under light anesthetic, and transmitter tags were attached to their backs. After being left for three days to acclimatize, all eleven fish were tracked one at a time for a period of three consecutive days, each using acoustic telemetry. Actograms were produced and compared to the wind-induced noise levels, measured using a hydrophone at different locations within the experimental pen. (For more detailed descriptions of acoustic telemetry and actograms, see Research Methods at the end of the Notes section.) The sole were found to be more active at higher wind speeds. At low wind speeds, the fish moved slowly (2 to 3 cm s^{-1}) and infrequently. At wind speeds greater than 8 m s^{-1}, the fish moved more frequently and at a higher speed (20 cm s^{-1}).

       One interesting aspect of how this research compares with other similar studies is that 8 m s^{-1} appears to be the critical wind speed at which the behavior of fish is significantly altered. Perhaps this is the speed at which the wind really begins to influence the underwater world.

72   **". . . scientists have estimated that each cubic mile of sky may contain as many as twenty-five million insects . . ."** Rothenberg, D. & Pryor, W. J. (2003). *Writing on Air.* Cambridge, MA: MIT Press.

73   **"There is some evidence that fish too are able to use the direction of swells to find their way around . . ."** Cook, P. H. (1984). Directional information from surface swell: some possibilities. In *Mechanisms of Migration in Fishes,* McLeave, J. D., Arnold, G. P., Dodson, J. J. & Neill, W. H., eds. New York: Plenum Press, 79–101.

       Cook looked at the possibility of fish using wind-driven surface swell as a navigational aid. The magnitude and direction of the swell can be predicted seasonally in different parts of the world. For example, in the North Atlantic between 40°N and 60°N, the swell heads eastward almost constantly. Cook noted that the Polynesian islanders used this reliable information effectively as a rough navigational aid for centuries. The movement at the surface affects the water for some distance below it.

Cook suggested that fish sufficiently close to the surface would be moved by such waves. He noted that swimming in the direction of the wave decreased the frequency of these movements. Swimming in the opposite direction, on the other hand, would increase them. It is clear therefore that fish are likely to be aware of the direction in which they are swimming. Tracking research revealed that salmon swimming near the surface were found to move in the direction of the swell during periods of bad weather. He concluded that surface swell could indeed be a useful navigational aid to migrating fish.

73–74   **"This is summed up in one experiment in which a zoologist who fed his minnows in a special aquarium compartment would regularly blow a whistle . . ."** Von Frisch, K. (1938). The sense of hearing in fish. *Nature* 141: 8–11.

77   **"As mentioned earlier, one biologist found that minnows became excited as light levels fell below a certain level."** Harden Jones, F. R. (1956). The behaviour of minnows in relation to light intensity. *Journal of Experimental Biology* 33: 271–81.

82   **"One interesting experiment showed how turbid water changes the behavior of salmon . . ."** Gregory, R. S. (1993). Effect of turbidity on the predator avoidance behaviour of juvenile chinook salmon (*Oncorhynchus tshawytscha*). *Canadian Journal of Fisheries and Aquatic Sciences* 50(2): 241–46.

85   **"Research has even shown that rain can increase shark attacks on people."** Allen, T. B. (2001). *Shark Attacks: Their Causes and Avoidance.* New York: The Lyons Press, 44, 114 & 169.

85   **"Scientists studying sharks have found that they do not remain in the same place . . ."** Allen, T. B. (2001). *Shark Attacks: Their Causes and Avoidance.* New York: The Lyons Press, 44, 114 & 169.

Chapter 4

93   **"Studies carried out on the stomach contents of lake- and river-dwelling trout reveal a varied diet throughout the year."** Allen, K. R. (1938). Some observations on the biology of the trout (*Salmo trutta*) in Windermere. *Journal of Animal Ecology* 7(2): 333–49.

Humphries, C. F. (1936). An investigation of the profundal and sublittoral fauna of Windermere. *Journal of Animal Ecology* 5: 29–52.

Pentelow, F. T. K. (1932). The food of the brown trout (*Salmo trutta* L.). *Journal of Animal Ecology* 1(2): 101–7.

97 **"Research has shown that far more deaths can be attributed to severe floods ..."** Needham, P. R. & Jones, A. C. (1959). Flow, temperature, solar radiation, and ice in relation to activities of fishes in Sagehen Creek, California. *Ecology* 40(3): 465–74.

99 **"One study examined the stomach contents of stickleback and found that turbidity was a key factor influencing feeding rates."** Moore, J. W. & Moore, I. A. (1976). The basis of food selection in some estuarine fishes. Eels, *Anguilla anguilla* (L.), whiting, *Merlangius merlangus* (L.), sprat, *Sprattus sprattus* (L.) and stickleback, *Gasterosteous aculeatus* L. *Journal of Fish Biology* 9(5): 375–90.

Moore and Moore examined the stomach contents of four species of fish: eel, whiting, sprat, and stickleback. Obtaining their fish by filtering the cooling system of the Oldbury-on-Severn power station (England), they found that turbidity was a main factor influencing the feeding rates of the estuarine fish. Turbidity led some fish to feed closer to the surface at a depth where the light was adequate. Their study also showed that the degree to which the reduced visibility associated with turbidity affected feeding was species-specific. When examining the stomach contents of the stickleback, Moore and Moore found that the fish had empty stomachs despite the researchers' efforts to catch fish at different times and therefore, on at least one occasion, just after feeding. They captured some of the stickleback and took them back to the laboratory in an attempt to find out why their stomachs were empty. Although, unfortunately, this was never determined, the results of their experiments were of interest. The ability of the stickleback to detect food particles in both clear and turbid water was tested. In clear water, the prey was detected up to a maximum distance of 44 centimeters. In turbid water, this distance was reduced to 26 centimeters. The time taken to capture a prey item also increased with turbidity levels.

The eels were found to have an empty stomach during the winter. This was thought to be due to the comparatively quick reactions of their prey. Laboratory experiments revealed that the eels did not dash at their prey like other fish species. Instead, they crept up on their intended meal. The researchers found that the eels' slow approach meant that the prey did not react with the usual escape mechanism. The slower eels had a higher catch rate than the faster fish for this particular prey species (the sand shrimp, *Crangon vulgaris*). The eels were found to prefer feeding on slower items of prey such as benthic (bottom-dwelling) invertebrates as opposed to the faster fish. They would only become piscivorous in the absence of benthic invertebrates. Interestingly, burrowing worms were rarely found in fishes' stomachs. This was thought to be due to the worms' presence several centimeters below the substrate surface. It was suggested that the fish were unable to dig down this far. When feeding, eels were found to be highly selective, identifying their tiny, invertebrate prey items before consuming them. The eels were found to eat little or nothing when the temperature fell below 10° to 12°C, perhaps explaining their empty stomachs in the winter.

102 **"A study of the effects of bergs on the feeding behavior of river-dwelling trout ..."** Needham, P. R. & Jones, A. C. (1959). Flow, temperature, solar radiation, and ice in relation to activities of fishes in Sagehen Creek, California. *Ecology* 40(3): 465–74.

Studying the effects of ice on fish, Needham and Jones described two types of ice. Anchor ice forms on the bottom of streams and submerged objects. It is a mixture of ice and water of similar consistency to a Slush Puppie. Frazil ice is present in tiny particles within the water flow itself. This form of ice sticks to larger bodies of ice when the flow of the water causes them to collide. Anchor ice can almost completely block the flow of water as it builds up over time. Needham and Jones built an underwater observatory to view trout in a stream. They observed an occasion when snow from the banks was blown onto the stream by strong winds. So much of the snow was thrown over the stream that the surface was almost completely covered by it. This had the effect of cooling the water, increasing the quantity of frazil ice within the water, and as a result, the large masses of ice were seen to increase visibly due to the addition of frazil ice. Even in these conditions, trout were observed swimming between the large ice blocks and examining food particles presented by the slow flow of the river. The trout avoided the snow masses themselves but were seen to feed on the bottom around their edges. Surprisingly, the researchers observed an abundance of aquatic invertebrate life actively crawling over the ice. They described how, although the trout were feeding actively around these icebergs, they were considerably slower in their movements than they had been when observed during the summer months.

104 **". . . when it melts early, experiments have shown that fish grow less and are less likely to survive."** Lappalainen, J., Erm, V., Kjellman, J. & Lehtonen, H. (2000). Size-dependent winter mortality of age-0 pikeperch (*Stizostedion lucioperca*) in Përnu Bay, the Baltic Sea. *Canadian Journal of Fisheries and Aquatic Sciences* 57(2): 451–58.

Lappalainen, Erm, Kjellman, and Lehtonen noted that the death rate of young pike perch was related to the length of the ice cover during their first winter. When the ice cover melted early, the fish were exposed to harsher conditions (no longer protected from the winter by the ice) and thus grew less and were less likely to survive the winter. When the ice cover was prolonged, the fish attained better sizes and had a better survival chance.

Chapter 5

114 **"An interesting experiment using a simulated river to study how flow rate influences where salmon can be found . . ."** Giannico, G. R. & Healey, M. C. (1998). Effects of flow and food on winter movements of juvenile coho salmon. *Transactions of the American Fisheries Society* 127(4): 645–51.

Giannico and Healey noted that flow rate in their simulated river was enough to change emigration rates in young salmon. The faster the water flow, the greater the rate of downstream emigration. They also noted that when the river flow increased even only slightly, the salmon were more likely to migrate into the slack water habitats at the margins of the river. Interestingly, even the highest flow rates were still well below the maximum swimming speeds of the fish. This suggests that the fish chose to move away as the flow increased and were not simply washed downstream. Giannico and Healey also noted that as water temperatures decreased, the fish took cover behind boulders in an effort to reduce their energy costs. During periods of more average temperature, the fish were higher in the water and, as a result, were more easily displaced by heavy flow rates. They concluded that salmon are sensitive even to small changes in flow rate and suggested that this sensitivity could act as an early warning system, protecting the fish from scouring during very high flow rates.

115 **"Another study focused on the influence of flowing and still water on the feeding behavior of Atlantic salmon."** Rimmer, D. M. & Power, G. (1978). Feeding response of Atlantic salmon (*Salmo salar*) alevins in flowing and still water. *Journal of the Fisheries Research Board of Canada* 35(3): 329–32.

122 **"This is not to say that large lake trout do not consume flies on the surface, but research shows that smaller fish do so more readily."** Frost, W. E. & Brown, M. E. (1967). *The Trout: The Natural History of the Brown Trout in the British Isles*. London: Fontana New Naturalist (Collins).

125 **"One study found that trout could be positioned anywhere within an otherwise bare tank by providing the scantiest of cover."** Metcalfe, N. B., Huntingford, F. A. & Thorpe, J. E. (1986). Seasonal changes in feeding motivation of juvenile Atlantic salmon (*Salmo salar*). *Canadian Journal of Zoology* 64(11): 2439–46.

Research Methods

Acoustic telemetry uses a miniature ultrasonic transmitter that transmits acoustic messages to the antenna (four separate hydrophones). The time taken for the signal to reach each of the individual hydrophones is used to estimate the position of the transmitter. The position of individual fish can be mapped from the land or from a boat using handheld antennas (Jepsen, Pedersen, and Thorstad, 2000). The transmitter can be attached to the back of the fish (Bégout and Lagardère, 1995), inserted via the mouth into the stomach, or surgically implanted into the body cavity. Once the 3-minute surgical operation has been performed, slime from the body of the fish carefully rubbed over the wound provides protection (Nykänen, Huusko, and Mäki-Petäys, 2001). Experiments have shown that these tags do not affect the swimming activity, behavior, or growth rates of the fish (Bégout Anras, Bodaly, and McNicol, 1998; Nykänen, Huusko, and Mäki-Petäys, 2001). This method can also be used to measure the speed of surface currents by attaching a transmitter to a float and releasing it into the surface water (Lagardère, Bégout, Lafaye, and Villotte, 1994). Interestingly, the received signal decreased in strength for certain fish. This was found to be because they had been eaten, transmitter and all, by another fish. An experienced tracker would be able to determine whether the signal was coming from inside the fish or inside the fish's predator (Jepsen, Pedersen, and Thorstad, 2000).

Priede, Bagley, and Smith (1994) used baited mackerel attached to an unmanned submersible to feed transmitters to deep-sea fish. The fish were subsequently tracked.

Deoxygenation of water can be achieved by the addition of sodium sulphite and cobalt nitrate. The cobalt nitrate acts as a catalyst, speeding up the reaction between sulphite and oxygen to create sulphate and thus deoxygenate surrounding water (Alabaster and Robertson, 1961).

Principal components analysis (PCA) is a method of assessing dominance hierarchy in fish populations. Each fish is given points for position within the tank, food consumption, and social interactions. The totals of these scores provide a list of individual fish in order of dominance (Sloman, Taylor, Metcalfe, and Gilmour, 2001).

Position control can be used to ensure that a fish holds a certain position within an aquarium. Metcalfe, Huntingford, and Thorpe (1986) found that fish could be positioned anywhere within a bare fish tank. A square made from black insulating tape was attached to the side of the aquarium at a sufficient height above the floor of the tank to allow the fish to enter but low enough to provide the feel of cover. A similar-sized black square was then stuck to the floor of the aquarium beneath it. The fish would always be positioned with their heads facing into the current of water. During their experiments, the fish spent over 90 percent of their time with their heads under the cover of these shelters.

Electrofishing involves passing an electric current through a body of water. This current should be strong enough to stun the fish but not so strong that it kills the fish. Stunned fish can then be collected as they float to the surface. The fish recover after a few seconds (Egglishaw and Shackley, 1982). In order to get an accurate sample, seine nets can be placed at either end of the sample area to prevent fish from escaping (Erman, Andrews, and Yoder-Williams, 1988).

Automatic recorders can be used to measure fish locomotory activity when movement in the water, caused by the movement of the fish, moves a celluloid vane connecting and disconnecting a circuit. The number of times the circuit is disconnected or connected per unit time is used to measure locomotory activity (Harden Jones, 1956).

Demand feeding systems allow the fish to feed at will by biting a trigger positioned 10 centimeters below the water level. Each time the trigger is bitten, a feeder releases between 15 and 25 grams of food into the water while the exact time and date of each release of the trigger are recorded. The fish have to be trained to operate such a mechanism. This has been achieved by feeding the fish above the trigger until they learned to operate the system. This took two weeks (Anras, 1995). By placing the trigger 2 centimeters above water level, its accidental operation can be avoided (Boujard and Leatherland, 1992).

Scale reading can be used to determine the age and growth of fish. During the winter, the growth rate is low. During the summer, the growth rate increases. This leads to an increase or decrease in the calcium deposits laid down in ridges on the scales. These ridges are known as *circuli*. The comparatively thinly spaced circuli of winter (known as the *annulus*) can be used to count the number of years a fish has been alive and therefore its age. The thickness of these rings also provides valuable information about growth rates at particular stages within a fish's life cycle (Wingfield, 1940). Other calcified fish structures can be used in much the same way. Otoliths are found in the inner ear of fish. Each ear contains three, the largest of which is normally used for aging purposes. The advantage of otoliths is that they show a daily cycle of deposition as opposed to the seasonal one shown by scales. This daily cycle is of particular use in aging very young fish. For catfish, the pectoral spines can be used (Pegg and Pierce, 2001). The obvious disadvantage of the latter two methods is that the fish must be killed in order for its age to be determined.

Mark recapture is a method of estimating changes in fish population sizes. Fish are caught and marked by the addition of tags or by fin-clipping. The fish are then released. After a suitable period of time, the same area is fished, and the number of the marked fish recaptured provides information on the movements of individual fish within a population (Harcup, Williams, and Ellis, 1984).

Actograms are graphical representations of fish movements and lists of fish swimming speed. These are achieved by tagging the fish and recording their movement via the process of acoustic telemetry (Lagardère, Bégout, Lafaye, and Villotte, 1994).

Photocells can be used to monitor the movement of fish. As the fish moves, its activity breaks a series of light beams set within the aquarium. The number of times the light beam is broken per unit of time is recorded, and this is then used to calculate the relative speeds of locomotion (Reynolds and Casterlin, 1979).

Respirometers are used to measure an organism's oxygen uptake. The animal is placed into a chamber, and the oxygen uptake is measured (Wood, 1932).

Fish traps can be used to catch small fish. These traps consist of a cylinder of wire netting with two funnel-shaped openings, one at either end. The trap is baited with food and lowered into the water. Once the fish enter the trap, they find it difficult to get out. After several hours, the trap and its catch are pulled out of the water (Allen, 1935).

Angling with rod and line is often a good method of sampling fish populations (Young, 1999). Allen (1935) found that this method of sampling caught the largest fish. This method does have a disadvantage in that it only samples healthy, feeding fish.

Echo sounders send waves into the water from the surface and pick them up as they pass again after being reflected back at different depths by subsurface objects. It is then possible to determine the presence of fish and plankton as well as the structure of the lake, river, or sea bed (Dembiński, 1971).

Fin clipping can be used in order to allow the identification of individuals within a large group of fish. By excising the tips of fins in various combinations, researchers can recognize individuals. This method did not affect the behavior of the fish or their growth rates (Fausch, 1984).

Time-lapse video can be used to provide information about the exact locality of individual fish over a certain periodicity. Fowler, Jensen, Collins, and Smith (1999) used a time-lapse camera to monitor the position of pouting around an artificial reef in Poole Bay, Dorset, in England under varying water velocities.

Shuttle boxes can be used to determine the preferred temperature of a fish. A shuttle box comprises two cells interconnected by a plastic tube of adequate diameter for the fish to pass through. Separate pipes feed each box with water. One cell is "cold" and the other cell is "warm." The difference in temperature between the two cells is controlled by a computer and maintained at a constant 2°C. A photocell placed at either end of the connecting tube allows the computer to use the last beam to be broken to determine the location of the fish. When the fish is in the "cold" cell, the water temperature is lowered by the computer. The fish is able to move into the "warm" cell if the temperature becomes too low. If the fish is in the "warm" cell, the temperature is increased. In this way, the fish is able to behaviorally determine its temperature preference by "shuttling" (hence the name) between cells. The computer continuously monitors the preferred temperature of each fish.

Dawn and dusk can be simulated within a laboratory by using a timed dimmer that increases light intensity slowly in the morning for 30 minutes, at which point maximum light intensity is reached. Dusk is simulated by the 30-minute reduction of light intensity to darkness at the end of the simulated day. Alternatively, a shutter can be automatically passed in front of the light source over a defined period of time. This will reduce the light intensity slowly. When the shutter is pulled back, the light intensity is slowly increased (Sogard and Olla, 1996).

Plankton nets are used to collect samples of plankton from a body of water. They can be pulled horizontally or vertically to sample specific places within the water column.

The area of water sampled can be calculated from the diameter of the mouth of the net times the distance the net was dragged through the water. The mesh size can be altered to trap selected size ranges of plankton for analysis. For example, Janssen and Brandt (1980) used a size-0 mesh with a diameter of 0.571 millimeter to collect samples of Lake Michigan plankton.

Larval or juvenile fish are often used in the experiments as they are smaller and usually easier to obtain and maintain than the adult form. In some cases, the behavior of adult fish is different from that of the juveniles. A great deal of the research is aimed directly at the juveniles in order to assess the factors affecting their survival, as it is the survival of these individuals that will determine the size of the future population of their species (MacKenzie and Kiørboe, 1995).

Turbulence can be simulated under laboratory conditions using turbulence-generating apparatus.

REFERENCES

Adron, J. W., Grant, P. T. & Cowey, C. B. (1973). A system for the quantitative study of the learning capacity of rainbow trout and its application to the study of food preferences and behavior. *Journal of Fish Biology* 5(5): 625–36.

Aflalo, F. G., ed. (1906). *Fishermen's Weather, by Upwards of One Hundred Living Anglers*. London: Adam and Charles Black.

Alabaster, J. S. & Robertson, K. G. (1961). The effect of diurnal changes in temperature, dissolved oxygen and illumination on the behavior of roach (*Rutilus rutilus* (L.)), bream (*Abramis brama* (L.)) and perch (*Perca fluviatilis* (L.)). *Animal Behaviour* 9(3–4): 187–92.

Allen, K. R. (1935). The food and migration of the perch (*Perca fluviatilis*) in Windermere. *Journal of Animal Ecology* 4(2): 264–73.

Allen, K. R. (1938). Some observations on the biology of the trout (*Salmo trutta*) in Windermere. *Journal of Animal Ecology* 7: 333–49.

Allen, T. B. (2001). *Shark Attacks: Their Causes and Avoidance*. New York: The Lyons Press, 44, 114, 169.

Amundsen, P.-A., Bergersen, R., Huru, H. & Heggberget, T. G. (1999). Diel feeding rhythms and daily food consumption of juvenile Atlantic salmon in the river Alta, northern Norway. *Journal of Fish Biology* 54(1): 58–71.

Anras, M.-L. B. (1995). Demand-feeding behaviour of sea bass kept in ponds: diel and seasonal patterns, and influences of environmental factors. *Aquaculture International* 3(3): 186–95.

Anras, M.-L. B. and Lagardère, J.-P. (1998). Weather related variability. Consequences on the swimming activity of a marine fish. *Compte Rendus de l'Académie des Sciences—Série 3—Sciences de la Vie* 321(8): 641–48.

Aronson, L. R. (1971). Further studies on orientation and jumping behaviour in the Gobiid fish, *Bathygobius soporator*. *Annals of the New York Academy of Sciences* 188: 378–92.

Bagur, D. (2004). The influence of rain on the feeding behaviour of brown trout. *Trout News*. Publication of the Centre for Environment, Fisheries & Aquaculture Science (CEFAS). 37: 25–27.

Baras, E., Tissier, F., Philippart, J.-C. & Mélard, C. (1999). Sibling cannibalism among juvenile vundu under controlled conditions. II. Effect of body weight and environmental variables on the periodicity and intensity of type II cannibalism. *Journal of Fish Biology* 54(1): 106–18.

Bass, A. H. & McKibben, J. R. (2003). Neural mechanisms and behaviors for acoustic communication in teleost fish. *Progress in Neurobiology* 69: 1–26.

Bégout, M.-L. & Lagardère, J.-P. (1995). An acoustic telemetry study of seabream (*Sparus aurata* L.): first results on activity rhythm, effects of environmental variables and space utilization. *Hydrobiologia* 300–301: 417–23.

Bégout Anras, M.-L., Bodaly, R. A. & McNicol, R. (1998). Use of an acoustic beam actograph to assess the effects of external tagging procedure on lake whitefish swimming activity. *Transactions of the American Fisheries Society* 127(2): 329–35.

Bégout Anras, M.-L., Lagardère, J.-P. & Lafaye, J.-Y. (1997). Diel activity rhythm of seabass tracked in a natural environment: group effects on swimming patterns and amplitudes. *Canadian Journal of Fisheries and Aquatic Sciences* 54: 162–68.

Bevelhimer, M. S. & Marshall Adams, S. (1993). A bioenergetics analysis of diel vertical migration by Kokanee salmon, *Oncorhynchus nerka*. *Canadian Journal of Fisheries and Aquatic Sciences* 50: 2336–49.

Billett, D. S. M., Lampitt, R. S., Rice, A. L. & Mantoura, R. F. C. (1983). Seasonal sedimentation of phytoplankton to the deep-sea benthos. *Nature* 302(5908): 520–22.

Bleckmann, H. (1980). Reaction time and stimulus frequency in prey localization in the surface-feeding fish *Aplocheilus lineatus*. *Journal of Comparative Physiology* 140(2): 163–72.

Bone, Q., Marshall, N. B. & Blaxter, J. H. S. (1999). *Biology of Fishes: Tertiary Level Biology*. 2nd ed. Gloucestershire, UK: Stanley Thornes Ltd.

Boujard, T. & Leatherland, J. F. (1992). Demand-feeding behaviour and diel pattern of feeding activity in *Oncorhynchus mykiss* held under different photoperiod regimes. *Journal of Fish Biology* 40(4): 535–44.

Brown, A. L. (1987). *Freshwater Ecology*. London: Heinemann Educational Books.

Brown, C., Dunbar, R., Kacelnik, A., Kendrick, K., Gosling, S., Else, L. & Douglas, K. (2004). Animal minds: do animals have minds of their own, and if they do, what might they be like? *New Scientist* 12 June.

Brown, C., Laland, K., & Krause, J. (2006). *Fish Cognition and Behavior.* Cambridge: Blackwell Publishing.

Brown, G. E. & Smith, R. J. F. (1997). Conspecific skin extracts elicit antipredator responses in juvenile rainbow trout (*Oncorhynchus mykiss*). *Canadian Journal of Zoology* 75: 1916–22.

Brown, R. S., Power, G. & Beltaos, S. (2001). Winter movements and habitat use of riverine brown trout, white sucker and common carp in relation to flooding and ice break-up. *Journal of Fish Biology* 59(5): 1126–41.

Brown, R. S., Power, G., Beltaos, S. & Beddow, T. A. (2000). Effects of hanging ice dams on winter movements and swimming activity of fish. *Journal of Fish Biology* 57(5): 1150–59.

Butvill, D. B. (2003). Incredible mutating carp. *BBC Wildlife Magazine* 21(December): 30.

Caprio, J. (1975). High sensitivity of catfish taste receptors to amino acids. *Comparative Physiology and Biochemistry* 52A: 247–51.

Carrell, S. (2003). Escape of a million farmed fish threatens wild salmon. *The Independent* 3 August.

Castonguay, M., Rose, G. A. & Leggett, W. C. (1992). Onshore movements of Atlantic mackerel (*Scomber scombrus*) in the northern Gulf of St. Lawrence: associations with wind-forced advections of warmed surface waters. *Canadian Journal of Fisheries and Aquatic Sciences* 49(11): 2232–41.

Chapman, D. W. (1966). Food and space as regulators of salmonid populations in streams. *American Naturalist* 100(913): 345–57.

Cobcroft, J. M., Pankhurst, P. M., Hart, P. R. & Battaglene, S. C. (2001). The effects of light intensity and algae-induced turbidity on feeding behaviour of larval striped trumpeter. *Journal of Fish Biology* 59(5): 1181–97.

Cocking, A. W. (1959a). The effects of high temperatures on roach (*Rutilus rutilus*). I. The effects of constant high temperatures. *Journal of Experimental Biology* 36: 203–16.

Cocking, A. W. (1959b). The effects of high temperatures on roach (*Rutilus rutilus*). II. The effects of temperature increasing at a known constant rate. *Journal of Experimental Biology* 36: 217–26.

Cook, P. H. (1984). Directional information from surface swell: some possibilities. In *Mechanisms of Migration in Fishes*, McLeave, J. D., Arnold, G. P., Dodson, J. J. & Neill, W. H., eds. New York: Plenum Press, 79–101.

Craig, J. F. (1977). Seasonal changes in the day and night activity of adult perch, *Perca fluviatilis* L. *Journal of Fish Biology* 11(2): 161–66.

Dawkins, M. S. (1998). *Through Our Eyes Only? The Search for Animal Consciousness*. Oxford: Oxford University Press.

Dembiński, W. (1971). Vertical distribution of vendace *Coregonus albula* L. and other pelagic fish species in some Polish lakes. *Journal of Fish Biology* 3(3): 341–57.

Edwards, C. A. & Bohlen, P. J. (1996). *Biology and Ecology of Earthworms*. London: Chapman & Hall, 60–63 & 102–7.

Egglishaw, H. J. & Shackley, P. E. (1982). Influence of water depth on dispersion of juvenile salmonids, *Salmo salar* L. and *S. trutta* L., in a Scottish stream. *Journal of Fish Biology* 21(2): 141–55.

Egglishaw, H. J. & Shackley, P. E. (1980). Survival and growth of salmon, *Salmo salar* (L.), planted in a Scottish stream. *Journal of Fish Biology* 16(5): 565–84.

Egglishaw, H. J. & Shackley, P. E. (1977). Growth, survival and production of juvenile salmon and trout in a Scottish stream, 1966–75. *Journal of Fish Biology* 11(6): 647–72.

Elliott, J. M. (1987). Population regulation in contrasting populations of trout *Salmo trutta* in two lake district streams. *Journal of Animal Ecology* 56(1): 83–98.

Elliott, J. M. (1986). Spatial distribution and behavioral movements of migratory trout *Salmo trutta* in a lake district stream. *Journal of Animal Ecology* 55(3): 907–22.

Elliott, J. M. (1975a). Weight of food and time required to satiate brown trout, *Salmo trutta* L. *Freshwater Biology* 5(1): 51–64.

Elliott, J. M. (1975b). Number of meals in a day, maximum weight of food consumed in a day and maximum rate of feeding for brown trout, *Salmo trutta* L. *Freshwater Biology* 5(3): 287–303.

Elliott, J. M. (1972). Rates of gastric evacuation in brown trout *Salmo trutta* L. *Freshwater Biology* 2(1): 1–18.

Erichsen Jones, J. R. (1952). The reactions of fish to water of low oxygen concentration. *Journal of Experimental Biology* 29: 403–16.

Erman, D. C., Andrews, E. D. & Yoder-Williams, M. (1988). Effects of winter floods on fishes in the Sierra Nevada. *Canadian Journal of Fisheries and Aquatic Sciences* 45(12): 2195–2200.

Fausch, K. D. (1984). Profitable stream positions for salmonids: relating specific growth rate to net energy gain. *Canadian Journal of Zoology* 62: 441–51.

FitzGerald, G. J. & Wootton, R. J. (1993). The behavioural ecology of sticklebacks. In *Behaviour of Teleost Fishes*, 2nd ed., Pitcher, T. J., ed. London: Chapman & Hall.

Fordham, S. E. & Trippel, E. A. (1999). Feeding behaviour of cod (*Gadus morhua*) in relation to spawning. *Journal of Applied Ichthyology* 15(1): 1–9.

Fountainbridge, P. (2003). Live fast, die young. *BBC Wildlife Magazine* September: 29.

Fowler, A. J., Jensen, A. C., Collins, K. J. & Smith, I. P. (1999). Age structure and diel activity of pouting on the Poole Bay artificial reef. *Journal of Fish Biology* 54(5): 944–54.

Frank, S. (1971). *The Pictorial Encyclopedia of Fishes*. London: Hamlyn.

Frost, W. E. & Brown, M. E. (1967). *The Trout: The Natural History of the Brown Trout in the British Isles*. London: Fontana New Naturalist (Collins).

Gardner, M. B. (1981). Effects of turbidity on feeding rates and selectivity of bluegills. *Transactions of the American Fisheries Society* 110(3): 446–50.

Giannico, G. R. & Healey, M. C. (1998). Effects of flow and food on winter movements of juvenile coho salmon. *Transactions of the American Fisheries Society* 127(4): 645–51.

Gooday, A. J. (2002). Biological responses to seasonally varying fluxes of organic matter to the ocean floor: a review. *Journal of Oceanography* 58(2): 305–32.

Gooday, A. J. & Turley, C. M. (1990). Responses by benthic organisms to inputs of organic material to the ocean floor: a review. *Philosophical Transactions of the Royal Society of London, Series A* 331(1616): 119–38.

Gregory, R. S. (1993). Effect of turbidity on the predator avoidance behaviour of juvenile chinook salmon (*Oncorhynchus tshawytscha*). *Canadian Journal of Fisheries and Aquatic Sciences* 50(2): 241–46.

Gunn, J. M. (1986). Behavior and ecology of salmonid fishes exposed to episodic pH depressions. *Environmental Biology of Fishes* 17(4): 241–52.

Hall, L. W., Pinkney, A. E., Horseman, L. O. & Finger, S. E. (1985). Mortality of striped bass larvae in relation to contaminants and water quality in a Chesapeake Bay tributary. *Transactions of the American Fisheries Society* 114(6): 861–68.

Halvorsen, M. & Stabell, O. B. (1990). Homing behaviour of displaced stream-dwelling brown trout. *Animal Behaviour* 39(6): 1089–97.

Harcup, M. F., Williams, R. & Ellis, D. M. (1984). Movements of brown trout, *Salmo trutta* L., in the river Gwyddon, South Wales. *Journal of Fish Biology* 24(4): 415–26.

Harden Jones, F. R. (1956). The behaviour of minnows in relation to light intensity. *Journal of Experimental Biology* 33: 271–81.

Harr, R. D. (1981). Some characteristics and consequences of snowmelt during rainfall in western Oregon. *Journal of Hydrology* 53: 277–304.

Hasler, A. D. & Scholz, A. T. (1983). *Olfactory Imprinting and Homing in Salmon: Investigations into the Mechanism of the Imprinting Process.* Berlin: Springer-Verlag.

Heath, S. E. (1999). *Animal Management in Disasters.* St. Louis, MO: Mosby, Chapters 4, 5, 6, 7 & 9.

Heggenes, J., Krog, O. M. W., Lindås, O. R., Dokk, J. G. & Bremnes, T. (1993). Homeostatic behavioural responses in a changing environment: brown trout (*Salmo trutta*) become nocturnal during winter. *Journal of Animal Ecology* 62(2): 295–308.

Helfman, G. S. (1989). Threat-sensitive predator avoidance in damselfish-trumpetfish interactions. *Behavioral Ecology and Sociobiology* 24: 47–58.

Hoare, D. J., Krause, J., Peuhkuri, N. & Godin, J.-G. J. (2000). Body size and shoaling in fish. *Journal of Fish Biology* 57(6): 1351–66.

Hollister, C. D. & McCave, I. N. (1984). Sedimentation under deep-sea storms. *Nature* 309(5965): 220–25.

Holmgren, K. & Appelberg, M. (2000). Size structure of benthic freshwater fish communities in relation to environmental gradients. *Journal of Fish Biology* 57(5): 1312–30.

Humphries, C. F. (1936). An investigation of the profundal and sublittoral fauna of Windermere. *Journal of Animal Ecology* 5: 29–52.

Huntingford, F. A., Wright, P. J., & Tierney, J. F. (1994). Adaptive variation in antipredator behaviour in threespine stickleback. In *The Evolutionary Biology of the Threespine Stickleback*, Bell, M. A. & Foster, S. A., eds. Oxford: Oxford University Press.

Huttula, T., Peltonen, A., Bilaletdin, Ä. & Saura, M. (1992). The effects of climatic change on lake ice and water temperature. *Aqua Fennica* 22(2): 129–42.

Jackson, D. A., Peres-Neto, P. R. & Olden, J. D. (2001). What controls who is where in freshwater fish communities—the roles of biotic, abiotic, and spatial factors. *Canadian Journal of Fisheries and Aquatic Sciences* 58(1): 157–70.

Janssen, J. & Brandt, S. B. (1980). Feeding ecology and vertical migration of adult alewives (*Alosa pseudoharengus*) in Lake Michigan. *Canadian Journal of Fisheries and Aquatic Sciences* 37(2): 177–84.

Jepsen, N., Pedersen, S. & Thorstad, E. (2000). Behavioural interactions between prey (trout smolts) and predators (pike and pikeperch) in an impounded river. *Regulated Rivers: Research & Management* 16(2): 189–98.

Jepsen, N., Koed, A. & Økland, F. (1999). The movements of pikeperch in a shallow reservoir. *Journal of Fish Biology* 54(5): 1083–93.

Kadri, S., Metcalfe, N. B., Huntingford, F. A. & Thorpe, J. E. (1995). What controls the onset of anorexia in maturing adult female Atlantic salmon? *Functional Ecology* 9(5): 790–97.

Kestin, S. (1997). Welfare of fish at slaughter. *Trout News*. Publication of the Centre for Environment, Fisheries & Aquaculture Science (CEFAS). 24: 42–44.

Kihara, K. & Shimada, A. M. (1988). Prey-predator interactions of walleye pollock *Theragra chalcogramma* and water temperature in the Bering Sea. *Bulletin of the Japenese Society of Scientific Fisheries* 54(7): 1131–35.

Kitchen, C. (2002). The flying flounder. *Daily Mail*, 30 October: 9.

Kruuk, H. & Tinbergen, N. (2003). *The Life of Niko Tinbergen and His Science of Animal Behaviour*. Oxford: Oxford University Press, 87.

Kupschus, K. & Tremain, D. (2001). Associations between fish assemblages and environmental factors in nearshore habitats of a subtropical estuary. *Journal of Fish Biology* 58(5): 1383–1403.

Kynard, B. E. (1978). Breeding behavior of a lacustrine population of threespine sticklebacks (*Gasterosteus aculeatus* L.). *Behaviour* 67(3–4): 178–207.

Lagardère, J.-P., Bégout, M.-L., Lafaye, J. Y. & Villotte J.-P. (1994). Influence of wind-produced noise on orientation in the sole (*Solea solea*). *Canadian Journal of Fisheries and Aquatic Sciences* 51(6): 1258–64.

Laland, K. N., Brown, C. & Krause, J. (2003). Learning in fishes: from three-second memory to culture. *Fish and Fisheries* 4(3): 199–202.

Lappalainen, J., Erm, V., Kjellman, J. & Lehtonen, H. (2000). Size-dependent winter mortality of age-0 pikeperch (*Stizostedion lucioperca*) in Pärnu Bay, the Baltic Sea. *Canadian Journal of Fisheries and Aquatic Sciences* 57(2): 451–58.

Lappalainen, J. & Lehtonen, H. (1997). Temperature habitats for freshwater fishes in a warming climate. *Boreal Environment Research* 2(1): 69–84.

Lappalainen, J. & Vinni, M. (2001). Movement of age-1 pikeperch under the ice cover. *Journal of Fish Biology* 58(2): 588–90.

Leach, S. D. & Houde, E. D. (1999). Effects of environmental factors on survival, growth, and production of American shad larvae. *Journal of Fish Biology* 54(4): 767–86.

Lehtonen, H. & Lappalainen, J. (1995). The effects of climate on the year-class variations of certain freshwater fish species. In *Climate Change & Northern Fish Populations: Proceedings of the Symposium on Climate Change and Northern Fish Populations*, Held in Victoria, British Columbia, 19–24 October, 1992, Beamish, R. J., ed. Ottawa, ON: NRC Research Press. 121: 37–44.

Liley, N. R. (1982). Chemical communication in fish. *Canadian Journal of Fisheries and Aquatic Sciences* 39: 22–35.

Lindstrøm, T. & Bergstrand, E. (1979). The habitat of perch, *Perca fluviatilis* L., on the outskirts of its Swedish distribution, lakes and lake reservoirs. *Reports from the Institute of Freshwater Research, Drottningholm* 58: 55–76.

Losey, G. S., Cronin, T. W., Goldsmith, T. H., Hyde, D., Marshall, N. J. & McFarland, W. N. (1999). The UV visual world of fishes: a review. *Journal of Fish Biology* 54(5): 921–43.

Love, J. A. (1990). *Sea Otters: The Soft Gold Rush.* London: Whittet Books, 37–50.

Lythgoe, J. N. & Northmore, D. P. M. (1973). Problems of seeing colours underwater. In *Color '73*. London: Adam Hilger, 77–98.

MacKenzie, B. R. & Kiørboe, T. (1995). Encounter rates and swimming behavior of pause-travel and cruise larval fish predators in calm and turbulent laboratory environments. *Limnology and Oceanography* 40(7): 1278–89.

MacKenzie, B. R., Miller, T. J., Cyr, S. & Leggett, W. C. (1994). Evidence for a dome-shaped relationship between turbulence and larval fish ingestion rates. *Limnology and Oceanography* 39(8): 1790–99.

Maes, J., Pas, J., Taillieu, A., Van Damme, P. A. & Ollevier, F. (1999). Diel changes in the vertical distribution of juvenile fish in the Zeeschelde Estuary. *Journal of Fish Biology* 54(6): 1329–33.

Magurran, A. E., Oulton, W. & Pitcher, T. J. (1985). Vigilant behaviour and shoal size in minnows. *Zeitschrift für Tierpsychologie* 67: 167–78.

McFarland, W. N. (1986). Light in the sea—correlations with behaviors of fishes and invertebrates. *American Zoologist* 26(2): 389–401.

McNicol, R. E., Bégout-Anras, M. L. & Scherer, E. (1999). Influence of light preferences on the avoidance responses of lake whitefish, *Coregonus clupeaformis*, to cadmium. *Environmental Biology of Fishes* 55(3): 295–306.

Megrey, B. A. & Hinckley, S. (2001). Effect of turbulence on feeding of larval fishes: a sensitivity analysis using an individual-based model. *ICES Journal of Marine Science* 58(5): 1015–29.

Metcalfe, N. B., Huntingford, F. A. & Thorpe, J. E. (1986). Seasonal changes in feeding motivation of juvenile Atlantic salmon (*Salmo salar*). *Canadian Journal of Zoology* 64(11): 2439–46.

Meyler, J. (1990). *Weather to Fish (or Game Fishing and the Elements)*. Bath, England: Bookcraft, 11–100.

Moore, J. W. & Moore, I. A. (1976). The basis of food selection in some estuarine fishes. Eels, *Anguilla anguilla* (L.), whiting, *Merlangius merlangus* (L.), sprat, *Sprattus sprattus* (L.) and stickleback, *Gasterosteous aculeatus* L. *Journal of Fish Biology* 9(5): 375–90.

Needham, P. R. & Jones, A. C. (1959). Flow, temperature, solar radiation, and ice in relation to activities of fishes in Sagehen Creek, California. *Ecology* 40(3): 465–74.

Nykänen, M., Huusko, A. & Mäki-Petäys, A. (2001). Seasonal changes in the habitat use and movements of adult European grayling in a large subarctic river. *Journal of Fish Biology* 58(2): 506–19.

Olla, B. L. & Davis, M. W. (1990). Behavioral responses of juvenile walleye pollock *Theragra chalcogramma* pallas to light, thermoclines and food: possible role in vertical distribution. *Journal of Experimental Marine Biology and Ecology* 135: 59–68.

Ottaway, E. M. & Forrest, D. R. (1983). The influence of water velocity on the downstream movement of alevins and fry of brown trout, *Salmo trutta* L. *Journal of Fish Biology* 23(2): 221–27.

Pavlov, D. S., Sadkovskii, R. V., Kostin, V. V. & Lupandin, A. I. (2000). Experimental study of young fish distribution and behaviour under combined influence of baro-, photo- and thermo-gradients. *Journal of Fish Biology* 57(1): 69–81.

Pedersen, J. & Hislop, J. R. G. (2001). Seasonal variations in the energy density of fishes in the North Sea. *Journal of Fish Biology* 59(2): 380–89.

Pegg, M. A. & Pierce, C. L. (2002). Fish community structure in the Missouri and Lower Yellowstone rivers in relation to flow characteristics. *Hydrobiologia* 479(1–3): 155–67.

Pegg, M. A. & Pierce, C. L. (2001). Growth rate responses of Missouri and Lower Yellowstone River fishes to a latitudinal gradient. *Journal of Fish Biology* 59(6): 1529–43.

Pentelow, F. T. K. (1932). The food of brown trout (*Salmo trutta*). *Journal of Animal Ecology* 1: 101–7.

Phillips, C. (1965). *The Captive Sea: Fabulous Stories of Marine Life in One of the World's Greatest Seaquariums.* London: Frederick Muller Limited.

Pires, A. M., Cowx, I. G. & Coelho, M. M. (1999). Seasonal changes in fish community structure of intermittent streams in the middle reaches of the Guadiana basin, Portugal. *Journal of Fish Biology* 54: 235–49.

Pitcher, T. J., ed. (1993). *Behaviour of Teleost Fishes.* 2nd ed. London: Chapman & Hall.

Pitcher, T. J. & House, A. C. (1987). Foraging rules for group feeders: forage area copying depends upon food density in shoaling goldfish. *Ethology* 76: 161–67.

Pliny. (1958). *Natural History.* Cambridge, MA: Harvard University Press.

Porter, M. J. R., Duncan, N., Handeland, S. O., Stefansson, S. O. & Bromage, N. R. (2001). Temperature, light intensity and plasma melatonin levels in juvenile Atlantic salmon. *Journal of Fish Biology* 58(2): 431–38.

Pough, F. H., Janis, C. M. & Heiser, J. B. (2002). *Vertebrate Life.* 6th ed. Upper Saddle River, NJ: Prentice Hall.

Pressley, P. H. (1981). Parental effort and the evolution of nest guarding tactics in the threespine stickleback, *Gasterosteus aculeatus* L. *Evolution* 35(2): 282–95.

Priede, I. G., Bagley, P. M. & Smith, K. L. (1994). Seasonal change in activity of abyssal demersal scavenging grenadiers *Coryphaenoides (Nematonurus) armatus* in the eastern North Pacific Ocean. *Limnology and Oceanography* 39(2): 279–85.

Raitaniemi, J. (1995). The growth of young pike in small Finnish lakes with different acidity-related water properties and fish species composition. *Journal of Fish Biology* 47(1): 115–25.

Raitaniemi, J., Rask, M. & Vuorinen, P. J. (1988). The growth of perch, *Perca fluviatilis* L., in small Finnish lakes at different stages of acidification. *Annales Zoologici Fennici* 25(3): 209–19.

Rask Møller, P., Nielsen, J. G. & Fossen, I. (2003). Patagonian toothfish found off Greenland. *Nature* 421: 599.

Rask, M., Vuorinen, P. J., Raitaniemi, J., Vuorinen, M., Lappalainen, A. & Peuranen, S. (1992). Whitefish stocking in acidified lakes: ecological and physiological responses. *Hydrobiologia* 243–44: 277–82.

Raymond, J. A. & Hassel, A. (2000). Some characteristics of freezing avoidance in two osmerids, rainbow smelt and capelin. *Journal of Fish Biology* 57(SUPA): 1–7.

Reader, J. P. & Dempsey, C. H. (1989). Episodic changes in water quality and their effects on fish. In *Acid Toxicity and Aquatic Animals*, Morris, R., Taylor, E. W. & Brown, D. J. A., eds. Society of Experimental Biology Seminar Series 34. Cambridge: Cambridge University Press.

Reebs, S. (2001). *Fish Behavior: In the Aquarium and in the Wild*. Ithaca, NY: Cornell University Press.

Reynolds, W. W. & Casterlin, M. E. (1979). Effect of temperature on locomotor activity in the goldfish (*Carassius auratus*) and the bluegill (*Lepomis macrochirus*): presence of an "activity well" in the region of the final preferendum. *Hydrobiologia* 65(1): 3–5.

Rimmer, D. M. & Power, G. (1978). Feeding response of Atlantic salmon (*Salmo salar*) alevins in flowing and still water. *Journal of the Fisheries Research Board of Canada* 35(3): 329–32.

Rimmer, D. M., Saunders, R. L. & Paim, U. (1985). Effects of temperature and season on the position holding performance of juvenile Atlantic salmon (*Salmo salar*). *Canadian Journal of Zoology* 63: 92–96.

Rokop, F. J. (1974). Reproductive patterns in the deep-sea benthos. *Science* 186(4165): 743–45.

Rørvik, K.-A., Skjervold, P. O., Fjæra S. O., Mørkøre, T. & Steien, S. H. (2001). Body temperature and seawater adaptation in farmed Atlantic salmon and rainbow trout during prolonged chilling. *Journal of Fish Biology* 59(2): 330–37.

Rosenthal, G. G., Evans, C. S. & Miller, W. L. (1996). Female preference for dynamic traits in the green swordtail, *Xiphophorus helleri*. *Animal Behaviour* 51(4): 811–20.

Rosseland, B. O., Kroglund, F., Staurnes, M., Hindar, K. & Kvellestad, A. (2001). Tolerance to acid water among strains and life stages of Atlantic salmon (*Salmo salar* L.). *Water, Air & Soil Pollution* 130(1–4): 899–904.

Rothenberg, D. & Pryor, W. J. (2003). *Writing on Air*. Cambridge, MA: MIT Press.

Rowland, W. J. (1995). Do female stickleback care about male courtship vigour? Manipulation of display tempo using video playback. *Behaviour* 132(13–14): 951–61.

Rowland, W. J. (1989a). Mate choice and the supernormality effect in female sticklebacks (*Gasterosteus aculeatus*). *Behavioral Ecology and Sociobiology* 24(6): 433–38.

Rowland, W. J. (1989b). The effects of body size, aggression, and nuptial colouration on competition for territories in male three-spined sticklebacks, *Gasterosteus aculeatus. Animal Behaviour* 37: 282–9.

Rudstam, L. G. & Magnuson, J. J. (1985). Predicting the vertical distribution of fish populations: analysis of cisco, *Coregonus artedii*, and yellow perch, *Perca flavescens. Canadian Journal of Fisheries and Aquatic Sciences* 42(6): 1178–88.

Scherer, E. (1992). Behavioral responses as indicators of environmental alterations: approaches, results, developments. *Journal of Applied Ichthyology* 8: 122–31.

Schultz, K. (2001). *North American Fishing: The Premier Guide to Angling in Freshwater and Saltwater.* Blue Ridge Summit, PA: Carlton Books.

Schurmann, H. & Steffensen, J. F. (1992). Lethal oxygen levels at different temperatures and the preferred temperature during hypoxia of the Atlantic cod, *Gadus morhua* L. *Journal of Fish Biology* 41(6): 927–34.

Scott, G. R., Sloman, K. A., Rouleau, C. & Wood, C. (2003). Cadmium disrupts behavioral physiological responses to alarm substance in juvenile rainbow trout (*Oncorhynchus mykiss*). *Journal of Experimental Biology* 206: 1779–90.

Seegrist, D. W. & Gard, R. (1972). Effects of floods on trout in Sagehen Creek, California. *Transactions of the American Fisheries Society* 101(3): 478–82.

Shipitalo, M. J. & Butt, K. R. (1999). Occupancy and geometrical properties of *Lumbricus terrestris* L. burrows affecting infiltration. *Pedobiologia* 43: 782–94.

Sloman, K. A., Taylor, A. C., Metcalfe, N. B. & Gilmour, K. M. (2001). Effects of an environmental perturbation on the social behaviour and physiological function of brown trout. *Animal Behaviour* 61(2): 325–33.

Sogard, S. M. & Olla, B. L. (1996). Food deprivation affects vertical distribution and activity of a marine fish in a thermal gradient: potential energy-conserving mechanisms. *Marine Ecology Progress Series* 133: 43–55.

Stander, P. E. & Albon, S. D. (1993). Hunting success of lions in a semi-arid environment. *Symposia of the Zoological Society of London* 65: 127–43.

Stanley, B. V. & Wootton, R. J. (1986). Effects of ration and male density on the territoriality and nest-building of male three-spined sticklebacks (*Gasterosteus aculeatus* L.). *Animal Behaviour* 34(2): 527–35.

Starr, M., Therriault, J.-C., Conan, G. Y., Comeau, M. & Robichaud, G. (1994). Larval release in a sub-euphotic zone invertebrate triggered by sinking phytoplankton particles. *Journal of Plankton Research* 16(9): 1137–47.

Sternberg, D. (1987). *Freshwater Gamefish of North America.* Upper Saddle River. NJ: Prentice Hall.

Stringer, C. (2006). Homo Britannicus: *The Incredible Story of Human Life in Britain.* London: Penguin Books.

Sutterlin, A. M. & Waddy, S. (1975). Possible role of the posterior lateral line in obstacle entrainment by brook trout (*Salvelinus fontinalis*). *Journal of the Fisheries Research Board of Canada* 32: 2441–46.

Swift, D. R. (1955). Seasonal variations in the growth rate, thyroid gland activity and food reserves of brown trout (*Salmo trutta* L.). *Journal of Experimental Biology* 32: 751–64.

Takegaki, T. (2001). Environmental factors affecting the spawning burrow selection by the gobiid *Valenciennea longipinnis*. *Journal of Fish Biology* 58: 222–29.

Tanck, M. W. T., Booms, G. H. R., Eding, E. H., Wendelaar Bonga, S. E. & Komen, J. (2000). Cold shocks: a stressor for common carp. *Journal of Fish Biology* 57(4): 881–94.

Tavolga, W. N. (1974). Signal/noise ratio and the critical band in fishes. *Journal of the Acoustical Society of America* 55(6): 1323–33.

Tavolga, W. N., Popper, A. N. & Fay, R. J., eds. (1981). *Hearing and Sound Communication in Fishes.* New York: Springer-Verlag, 455.

Taylor, J. F., North, B., Porter, M. J. R. & Bromage, N. R. (2002). Photoperiod manipulation can be used to improve growth rate and feeding efficiency in rainbow trout. *Trout News*. Publication of the Centre for Environment, Fisheries & Aquaculture Science (CEFAS). 33: 20–23.

Templeman, W. (1965). Mass mortalities of marine fishes in the Newfoundland area presumably due to low temperature. International Commission for the Northwest Atlantic Fisheries. *Special Publications* 6: 137–47.

Thyrel, M., Berglund, I., Larsson, S. & Näslund, I. (1999). Upper thermal limits for feeding and growth of 0+ Arctic charr. *Journal of Fish Biology* 55: 199–210.

Tyler, P. A. (1988). Seasonality in the deep sea. *Oceanography and Marine Biology: An Annual Review* 26: 227–58.

Utne-Palm, A. C. (1999). The effect of prey mobility, prey contrast, turbidity and spectral composition on the reaction distance of *Gobiusculus flavescens* to its planktonic prey. *Journal of Fish Biology* 54(6): 1244–58.

Valentinčič, T. & Caprio, J. (1997). Visual and chemical release of feeding behavior in adult rainbow trout. *Chemical Senses* 22(4): 375–82.

Van Orsdol, C. G. (1984). Foraging behavior and hunting success of lions in Queen Elizabeth National Park, Uganda. *African Journal of Ecology* 22: 79–99.

Von Frisch, K. (1938). The sense of hearing in fish. *Nature* 141: 8–11.

Von Frisch, K. (1938). Zur psychologie des fisch-schwarmes. *Die Naturwissenschaf-ten* 26(37): 601–6.

Von Frisch, K. (1941). Über einen Schreckstoff der Fischhaut und seine biologische Bedeutung. *Zeitschrift für Vergleichende Physiologie* 29: 46–145.

Ward, G. & FitzGerald, G. J. (1987). Male aggression and female mate choice in the threespine stickleback, *Gasterosteus aculeatus* L. *Journal of Fish Biology* 30(6): 679–90.

Warrer-Hansen, I. (2002). The importance of oxygen. *Trout News.* Publication of the Centre for Environment, Fisheries & Aquaculture Science (CEFAS). 34: 13–15.

Wilkinson, B. (1978). The agricultural effects of future climatic trends and policy implications on climatic change and European agriculture. Agriculture and climatic trends. ADAS & Ministry of Agriculture, *Fisheries and Food.* 3–7 & 21–27.

Wilson, E. O. (2003). *The Future of Life.* London: Abacus.

Wingfield, C. A. (1940). The effect of certain environmental factors on the growth of brown trout (*Salmo trutta* L.). *Journal of Experimental Biology* 17: 435–48.

Wood, A. H. (1932). The effect of temperature on the growth and respiration of fish embryos (*Salmo fario*). *Journal of Experimental Biology* 9: 271–76.

Woodhead, P. M. J. & Woodhead, A. D. (1955). Reactions of herring larvae to light: a mechanism of vertical migration. *Nature* 176: 349–50.

Wootton, R. J. (1998). *Ecology of Teleost Fishes.* 2nd ed. Fish & Fisheries Series 24. Dordrecht, The Netherlands: Kluwer Academic Publishers.

Young, M. K. (1999). Summer diel activity and movement of adult brown trout in high-elevation streams in Wyoming, U.S.A. *Journal of Fish Biology* 54: 181–89.

INDEX

Page numbers in *italics* refer to figures. Page numbers with an "n" refer to endnotes.